Miami

Text by Joann Biondi
Photography by Tony Arruza

Voyageur Press

Edited by Todd R. Berger
Designed by Andrea Rud
Printed in Hong Kong

00 01 02 03 04 5 4 3 2 1

Library of Congress Cataloging-in-Publication Data
Biondi, Joann.
    Miami / text by Joann Biondi ; photography by Tony Arruza.
        p. cm. — (Citylife pictorial guides)
    Includes bibliographical references and index.
    ISBN 0-89658-445-3 — ISBN 0-89658-498-4 (alk. paper)
      1. Miami (Fla.)—Pictorial works. 2. Miami (Fla.)—Guidebooks. I. Arruza, Tony. II. Title. III. Series.

    F319.M6 B55 2000
    917.59'3810464—dc21   00-026018

Distributed in Canada by Raincoast Books, 9050 Shaughnessy Street, Vancouver, B.C. V6P 6E5

Published by Voyageur Press, Inc.
123 North Second Street, P.O. Box 338, Stillwater, MN 55082 U.S.A.
651-430-2210, fax 651-430-2211
books@voyageurpress.com
www.voyageurpress.com

Educators, fundraisers, premium and gift buyers, publicists, and marketing managers: Looking for creative products and new sales ideas? Voyageur Press books are available at special discounts when purchased in quantities, and special editions can be created to your specifications. For details contact the marketing department at 800-888-9653.

Page 1: *A palm tree waving in the ocean breeze in front of the Leslie Hotel on Ocean Drive.*

Facing page: *A kinte cloth hat and a happy face.*

Page 4: *Tequesta Indian by M. Carboney adds human scale to a downtown skyscraper.*

Page 5: *Fresh papaya, pineapple, banana, kiwi, oranges, and avocados ready for sale.*

Contents

Introduction   7

A Bustling Metropolis   15

A Sensual Oasis   31

The Deco Lifestyle   49

Latin Nights and Daytime Diversions   65

A Tapestry of People and Places   79

Index   94

Where to Go for More Information   95

About the Author and Photographer   96

Introduction

"Miami seemed not a city at all but a tale, a romance of the tropics,
a kind of waking dream in which any possibility could and
would be accommodated."
—Joan Didion, *Miami,* 1987

It's only when I leave Miami and travel to other corners of America that I realize how foreign, flamboyant, and exotic my hometown really is. Not long ago while visiting my sister in upstate New York I found myself continually fiddling with the car radio searching for the salsa music and Spanish-speaking DJs I'm accustomed to listening to while driving—but they were nowhere to be found. On another trip, I was totally baffled when a live rhythm-and-blues band at an art festival in downtown Denver started jamming and not one person in the crowd shook their shoulders or shimmied their hips. And then there was the time I walked into a grocery store in Ohio and asked a produce boy if he had any plantains, starchy green bananas that are salted and fried and eaten like

potatoes back home in Miami. The produce boy looked at me and said, "Lady, I've never heard of plantains." After I described them, he added, "The only bananas we sell are the kind you eat with corn flakes and milk."

Whenever I land at Miami International Airport, I let out a heavy sigh, click my heels together three times, and like Dorothy say, "There's no place like home." The shoulder-to-shoulder mass of humanity that greets me includes Cubans, Nicaraguans, Peruvians, Jamaicans, Venezuelans, Haitians, Puerto Ricans, Salvadorans, Hondurans, Brazilians, St. Lucians, Argentineans, Chileans, Bahamians, Trinidadians, Colombians, Dominicans, and Ecuadorians. In the twenty or so years that I have made Miami home base, I've had my share of frustrations with life in

Above: *Multilayered Miccosukee Indian patchwork fabric, the only craft indigenous to Miami.*

Facing page: *The bright city lights reflect off the Miami River.*

the city—crime, traffic jams, corrupt politicians, August heat, and merciless hurricanes—but not once have I ever thought that Miami is a boring, bland, or banal place to live.

Miami is without a doubt the most "foreign" of U.S. cities. A recent U.S. Census Bureau poll revealed that it has a larger percentage (60 percent) of foreign-born residents than any other city in America. San Diego came in second with 42.6 percent and New York City third with 42.2 percent. Look in the Miami telephone directory and you'll find over 9,700 listings for the name Rodriguez, and 8,800 for Gonzales. Look up Smith and you'll find 2,300, and Jones, a mere 1,200.

Although some Miamians complain about the "foreigners" who have taken over their city, it is in fact the vast infusion of immigrant optimism that has given Miami its vibrant edge and unique sense of place in recent years. Here, people drive fast and arrive late. Here, people dress provocatively and dance until dawn. Here, people eat ripe mangos for breakfast and barbecue whole pigs in their backyards for dinner. Here, an ex-president of Panama sits in jail and newly arrived Russian mobsters cut deals on cellular phones. Here, yuccas (young upscale Cuban-Americans) crank up their air conditioning so that it's cool enough to light their fireplaces and puff on expensive contraband Cuban cigars.

During a typical visit to Miami a tourist is likely to spot a scantily clad supermodel posing for photographers, an Orthodox rabbi walking to temple in a long black coat, a Jamaican "Rastaman" selling freshly squeezed wheat-grass juice on a street corner, a Haitian master drummer performing under a full moon, a Miccosukee Indian wrestling an alligator, a drag queen on Rollerblades cruising down Ocean Drive, and a flamenco dancer working up a sweat as she dances at a bustling outdoor café. In Miami, an interesting encounter is right around the next corner.

Made up of about thirty different municipalities, Greater Miami, as it is often called, includes the island of Miami Beach and sits inside Miami-Dade County. Greater Miami sprawls over two thousand square miles, and has a population of about two million people. Although English is the "official" language, Spanish is the native tongue of most people who live here.

The Birth of a City

The story that explains Miami's diversity is a short one. For centuries before 1513, when Spanish explorer Juan Ponce de León sailed into Miami's Biscayne Bay searching for the Fountain of Youth, the Seminole people inhabited the virgin local landscape. They worked with tools made from seashells and ate wild game found in the nearby wetlands. In the mid-1500s, the first of the Spanish conquistadors came ashore and tried unsuccessfully to subdue the Seminoles and take over their land. Then came the French and the British who were also interested in south Florida's prospects. In 1763 the French and Indian War ended with Florida a British colony, but shortly after that Britain decided to swap with Spain and traded Florida for the nearby Bahama Islands.

By the 1800s, Florida was a haven for runaway slaves fleeing the oppression in other parts of the South, and in 1821 the United States gained control of the peninsula. Soon after, Americans began claiming land along the banks of the Miami River. From 1835 to 1857, a series of Indian attacks occurred, the most noted of which was the Dade Massacre of 1835, in which Major Francis L. Dade (for whom the county is named) was killed.

During the 1860s and 1870s, the first of many northern developers, whose names are now immortalized in local street signs, began to gobble up local real estate. William B. Brickell from Ohio bought land on the Miami River; Brickell Avenue is now one of the sleekest and most expensive streets in the city. Ralph M. Munroe of New York's Staten Island settled into what would later become the eclectic neighborhood called Coconut Grove. Bahamians, with their tropical know-how and tolerance for heat, came over to help build the city. Julia Tuttle, daughter of early settler Ephraim T. Sturtevant, played a pivotal role in this part of Miami's development. She convinced Standard Oil magnate Henry M. Flagler to extend his railroad from Palm Beach to Miami. In the cold winter of 1894–95, when Palm Beach was beset with frost, Tuttle sent Flagler a bouquet of fresh Miami orange blossoms. Although only seventy miles to the south, Miami has considerably milder winters than Palm Beach. Flagler, seduced by Miami's warm possibilities, rolled his train into town in 1896, the same year Miami officially became a city.

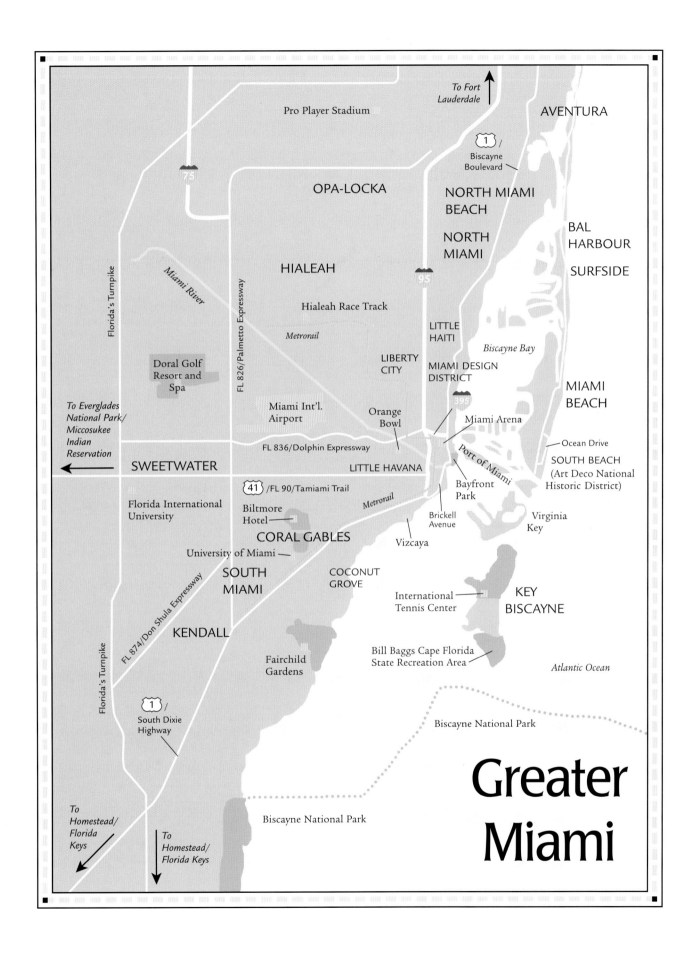

Pro Player Stadium

To Fort Lauderdale

AVENTURA

1 / Biscayne Boulevard

OPA-LOCKA

NORTH MIAMI BEACH

NORTH MIAMI

BAL HARBOUR

SURFSIDE

Florida's Turnpike

Miami River

75

HIALEAH

FL 826/Palmetto Expressway

Hialeah Race Track

Metrorail

LITTLE HAITI

95

Biscayne Bay

Doral Golf Resort and Spa

LIBERTY CITY

MIAMI DESIGN DISTRICT

MIAMI BEACH

To Everglades National Park/ Miccosukee Indian Reservation

Miami Int'l. Airport

Orange Bowl

395

Miami Arena

Ocean Drive

SOUTH BEACH (Art Deco National Historic District)

FL 836/Dolphin Expressway

SWEETWATER

LITTLE HAVANA

Port of Miami

41 /FL 90/Tamiami Trail

Metrorail

Bayfront Park

Florida International University

Biltmore Hotel

Brickell Avenue

Virginia Key

CORAL GABLES

Vizcaya

University of Miami

SOUTH MIAMI

COCONUT GROVE

International Tennis Center

KEY BISCAYNE

KENDALL

FL 874/Don Shula Expressway

Florida's Turnpike

Fairchild Gardens

Bill Baggs Cape Florida State Recreation Area

Atlantic Ocean

1 / South Dixie Highway

Biscayne National Park

To Homestead/ Florida Keys

Biscayne National Park

To Homestead/ Florida Keys

Greater Miami

The early 1900s witnessed modest growth for the area. Government Cut, which later became the Port of Miami and the largest cruise port in the world, was dredged. Miami Beach became a city, and holiday hotels sprouted up along the oceanfront like mushrooms. And America's upper class—people like James Deering, who built the mansion known as Vizcaya—started to construct lavish vacation homes on waterfront properties.

America's Playground

The Roaring Twenties brought a rush of hungry land developers who carved out communities like the Mediterranean-inspired city of Coral Gables, where the University of Miami was founded in 1926. But the 1920s also brought one of the most brutal hurricanes ever to hit the city. Boats were grounded, buildings demolished, and over one hundred people were killed in the "Big One" of 1926. Another monster hurricane would follow in 1935. But Miami rebounded, and in the late 1930s the city flourished again. This was the era of the great Art Deco hotels that would make the southern end of Miami Beach famous throughout the world. Over five hundred of these whimsical, cotton-candy structures were built—all with the Deco details of geometric patterns, racing stripes, neon lights, glass blocks, and pastel colors of pink, turquoise, lavender, and lime green. Tourists flocked to the faddish and playful hotels and danced to the big band sounds that filled the oceanside streets.

During World War II, many of these pretty hotels were transformed into hospitals and barracks for the thousands of U.S. soldiers who were stationed in Miami for military training. The war was actually not so far away from this pastel paradise: In the waters off the Florida coast, German submarines roamed the deep. When the war ended, Miami Beach returned to its status as "America's playground" and ground zero for many of the country's most notorious mobsters who grew rich on illegal gambling. Elderly Jews, fleeing the bitter-cold winters of the Northeast, also began settling in the area.

The 1950s brought more tourism growth to Miami. This time the hotels being built in the middle of Miami Beach were large and luxurious with ornate chandeliers, cool marble floors, and an overall atmosphere of opulence. The Fontainebleau and Eden Roc Hotels became known for their

A good-to-the-last-puff Cuban cigar.

pleasure-packed vacations catering to an elite class of tourists. Air conditioning became a staple rather than a luxury, and the area's population reached one million.

Enter Fidel

The end of the 1950s, however, brought a drastic change to Miami. On the Caribbean island of Cuba, a brazen revolutionary with an unruly black beard seized power in 1959. This man would eventually have as much of an impact on life in Miami as he had on Havana. President Fidel Castro, declaring himself a socialist, sent shock waves through the Western Hemisphere. By confiscating property and nationalizing island businesses, he caused many of Cuba's most affluent citizens to flee the country. Nearby Miami, with its similar climate, seemed a natural destination for the political refugees. In the years that followed, hundreds of thousands of Cubans seeking political asylum boarded "freedom flights" to Miami, thus planting the seed that would eventually transform Miami from a small, southern city famous for its sun-and-fun mentality into a

Miami's multicultural makeup is evident in every nook and cranny of the city.

bustling and cosmopolitan metropolis known as the capital of Latin America.

In 1961, A CIA-organized attempt to overthrow Castro and take over Cuba, known as the Bay of Pigs invasion, failed and left many expatriate Cubans in Miami frustrated. It was followed by the 1962 Cuban Missile Crisis, which fostered the threat of nuclear war with the Soviet Union and put the entire world on edge. The tense confrontation ended when President John F. Kennedy promised that the United States would not again try to invade Cuba, and the Soviets agreed to remove their missiles from the island. Castro retained control of his country, and Miami's Cuban-exile community now had to face the fact that they were not likely to be going home soon; any hope of a family reunion meant that their relatives would have to join them on U.S. soil.

Throughout the 1960s, Cuban exiles settled into a once "Anglo" neighborhood west of downtown Miami and began calling it Little Havana. Eventually, their presence—as well as their influence—spread to all parts of the city. Since many of the first-wave Cuban immigrants were members of the professional and entrepreneurial class, many brought with them valuable skills and remnants of past family wealth that enabled them to set up professions and small businesses—cigar factories, coffee shops, car lots, cafeterias—and cater to the exile community.

It was this first wave of energetic Cubans that helped make Miami a predominantly Hispanic city that would in time draw thousands more immigrants from throughout Central and South America. They came because of the lack of opportunities in their own countries, and the ease with which they could settle in the local community and find a job without having to be able to speak English.

The 1970s started out on a positive note for Miami. The Miami Dolphins football team brought championship pride to the city, President Richard M. Nixon vacationed on Key Biscayne, and the Cuban community seemed to assimilate into life in the United States. But the economic recession that plagued the country in the mid-1970s created hard times for Miami: Unemployment rose to 13 percent, major downtown construction projects were abandoned, and Miami's international banking community was hit with financial problems.

Around this time, thousands of Haitian immigrants started sailing to Miami in rickety wooden boats in search of a better life. Their plight—escaping the severe poverty and iron-fisted dictatorship of their Caribbean homeland—was understandable to Miamians, but since they were not fleeing a communist country, their entry into the United States was not as warmly welcomed by the authorities as was that of the Cuban immigrants.

Miami's African-American community was most affected by the recession. The community was already burdened by widespread poverty, and many African-Americans lost out on jobs that were taken by recent Hispanic immigrants. With Spanish language skills becoming necessary for employment, native Spanish speakers had a natural advantage, and blacks became even more marginalized by the system.

The Turbulent 1980s

The year 1980 will likely be remembered as Miami's worst. A white police officer charged with the slaying of a black insurance salesman was acquitted by a jury. The city's black community was outraged, and the largely black neighborhood of Liberty City erupted in violence. The riots ended with eighteen people dead and property damage totaling $100 million. Later that year, President Fidel Castro allowed 125,000 Cubans to leave the island in a massive boatlift from the Cuban port of Mariel. At first, Miami Cubans were jubilant at being reunited with relatives, but the U.S. government later learned that many of those "Marielitos" were actually convicted criminals and mental hospital patients whom Castro wanted to get rid of. Shortly thereafter, *Time* magazine published its infamous cover story on Miami titled, "Paradise Lost," a scathing portrait of a city overrun with crime, drugs, and racial tensions.

Also in 1980, the body of the assassinated former president of Nicaragua, Anastasio Somoza Debayle, was buried in a Little Havana cemetery. Many Nicaraguan refugees fleeing the leftist Sandinista takeover of their Central American country immigrated to Miami. Non-Hispanic whites left the area in search of a more "American" place to live, some with bumper stickers on their cars stating, "Will the last American leaving Miami please bring the flag?" This

tidal wave of "white flight" had a Diaspora effect on the city.

During the 1980s, drug smugglers known locally as "cocaine cowboys" began infiltrating the city. The illegal drug-smuggling industry was said to pump over $10 billion a year into the local economy, and many area bankers rarely questioned the huge amounts of money deposited into their businesses. Real estate brokers didn't blink at the boxes of cash that were often used to buy luxury homes and neither did the car dealers who specialized in selling bulletproof sedans. During this time, the sale of handguns soared and so did the city's murder rate. Bodies stuffed into the trunks of cars became a virtually everyday occurrence. In 1984 there were no less than seventeen double murders, five triple slayings, and a gruesome quintuple killing—all related to the sale of illegal drugs. In 1986 *Miami Herald* reporter Edna Buchanan won the coveted Pulitzer Prize for documenting more than five thousand violent deaths in her sixteen-year tenure at the paper. Edna, as she is known locally, would go on to become a much-celebrated murder mystery novelist.

But the mid-1980s also brought the beginnings of a new image for the city. The weekly television series *Miami Vice* turned Miami's crime statistics into a pastel-perfect rock music video of glamour and intrigue. At first, city officials were worried that the images of violence would have a damaging public-relations effect on the city's tourism industry. But later, when the glossy, Casablanca-in-the-tropics images of seaside lushness, beautiful women, fast cars, neon lights, and the dramatic downtown skyline were branded into the minds of television viewers around the world, opinions changed.

It was soon realized that *Miami Vice* was giving an essential boost to the local economy. Miami's crime-ridden reputation was no longer an obstacle to overcome; city leaders now considered Miami's fast-lane image desirable, enticing, and even "cool." Tourists from around the world, eager to experience a tamer version of the city's edginess, came to seek it out, and Miami became one of the most-talked-about cities in America.

The 1980s also brought Miami's first Cuban-

Coral Gables Congregational Church against a true-blue Miami sky.

Playing a game of dominoes, a favorite Miami pastime, in Little Havana.

born mayor, a new professional basketball team, and a rendezvous for President Ronald Reagan and Pope John Paul II in the gardens of Vizcaya. And, it brought the renaissance of the Art Deco hotels on South Beach, totally transforming this rundown neighborhood into a haven for trendsetters from around the world. Miami entered the 1990s with a renewed identity and a great sense of pride. The *New York Times* reported that Miami had the "richest cultural life of any city in the southeastern United States." The city's music and film industries expanded. Celebrities moved into town and spent millions of dollars renovating old mansions. The first Summit of the Americas brought heads of state from North and South America together to discuss the future of the Western Hemisphere. And a World Series baseball championship united the locals and surprised the country.

But a series of incidents threatened to wreak havoc once again: A visit by Nelson Mandela turned into a political circus when the Cuban community chastised him for his friendship with Fidel Castro; Hurricane Andrew leveled a mean swipe through the southern parts of the city; a series of tourist shootings terrified the local tourism industry; a slew of political scandals embarrassed city hall and sent a few city managers to prison; the brazen murder of Gianni Versace tarnished a piece of posh Ocean Drive. But Miami, the "Teflon city," didn't take long to bounce back.

The Face of the Future

New Year's 2000 was ushered in with a sizzling Latin music concert by local sweetheart and international diva Gloria Estefan at the newly opened American Airlines Arena. And as the city gently slides forward into the new millennium, it is full of confidence and promise.

While immigration woes continue to challenge the city—case in point the commotion over six-year-old castaway Elian Gonzalez—ethnic diversity has woven itself into the very nature of Miami. Successful Latino role models are not in short supply, and the Cuban immigrants of yesterday are now the movers-and-shakers of the city. Today, the mayors of the city and the county, the county police chief and county state attorney, the president of the largest bank, the president of the local state university, the owner of the largest real estate development company, the managing partner of the largest law firm, and nearly half of Miami-Dade County's twenty-seven-member delegation in the state legislature are either Cuban-born or of Cuban descent. Miami Cubans have put down deep roots in this community; recent polls have shown that fewer than 30 percent of the six hundred thousand Cuban-Americans living in Miami-Dade County say that they would like to return to Cuba once Fidel Castro is no longer in power and there is a change in the type of government on the island.

Once mocked for being a hot-tempered playground, Miami, with its mostly Latino population, is a harbinger of things to come for the rest of the country. Latinos are the fastest-growing ethnic group in the United States. In 1990 they represented about 15 percent of the total U.S. population. Based on current trends, the U.S. Census Bureau predicts a 75 percent increase in the Latino population by the year 2015, and an overall Latino population of ninety-six million by the year 2050. Many demographers and sociologists are taking a serious look at Miami today, because they see it as a valuable testing ground for what many other U.S. cities will look like in the next few decades.

While there are still many people who look at Miami and say, "This is not America," they are dead wrong. While giving a poetry reading in Miami recently, U.S. Poet Laureate Robert Pinsky told a jam-packed auditorium, "Miami is a more intense version of the United States itself." Miami is indeed America, and it is the modern, multicultural face of the future.

A Bustling Metropolis

"I consider Miami the cultural and economic capital of the Carribbean
and Latin America. And I love it for that. It's vibrant. It's alive.
And it's so multicultural."
—Jimmy Buffett, singer, in an interview in the *Miami Herald*, March 30, 1997

Above: *Already dense with high-rise development, downtown Miami is on the brink of yet another build-ing boom to take place early in the new millennium. Projects valued at nearly $3 billion are currently on the drawing boards, including new luxury residential, retail, corporate, and hotel developments. Spurred by low interest rates and a desire to base Latin American operations here, international developers are flocking to the city.*

Facing page: *Palm Island with the MacArthur Causeway, the Port of Miami, and the downtown skyline in the background. A lush exclusive residential enclave, Palm Island is the place where gangster Al Capone lived in the 1940s when he and his cronies ran illegal gambling casinos in Miami Beach. Many of the homes here have yachts moored in their backyards along with their own seaplane berths. The Port of Miami, the "cruise ship capital of the world," is home to twelve state-of-the-art terminals and eighteen cruise ships, accommodating over three million passengers a year who sail off on cruises to the Caribbean, Latin America, Europe, and the Far East.*

Above: *Crammed with stores selling luggage, clothing, jewelry, shoes, cameras, sporting goods, and electronics, downtown Miami is a shopper's paradise, particularly for residents of South America and the Caribbean. Many make trips to Miami several times a year just to load up on supplies. According to the Greater Miami Convention & Visitors Bureau, over three million Latin American tourists—mostly from Brazil, Argentina, Chile, Colombia, Venezuela, and Peru—visit the Miami area each year, pumping over three billion dollars into the local economy.*

Left: *The pretty pink sign that welcomes visitors to Bayside Marketplace. One of the most visited tourist attractions in Miami, Bayside Marketplace is a festive, sixteen-acre, open-air extravaganza of over 150 shops, restaurants, and attractions including Hard Rock Café. In a prime waterfront location, it has hundreds of boat docks that are used for both private and commercial crafts. In addition to the larger chain stores, the marketplace has dozens of unique boutiques and kiosks with treasures from around the world. It also has plenty of free live entertainment—jugglers, mimes, steel drum bands, flamenco dancers, salsa musicians—day and night. If these diversions aren't enough for visitors, romantic gondola rides, fishing excursions, waterfront sightseeing tours, catamaran rides, and disco dancing cruises are also available.*

Above left, top photo: *Built in 1925, this strikingly beautiful Mediterranean revival building on Biscayne Boulevard is known as the Freedom Tower. From 1962 to 1974, recently arrived Cuban refugees were taken here to process their immigration papers, hence the name. Originally built as the home of the now-defunct Miami News and designed to resemble the fifteenth-century Giralda tower in Seville, Spain, the Freedom Tower is often thought of as Miami's Statue of Liberty. From 1975 to 1987 the building sat empty and in tatters until a wealthy Saudi Arabian sheik bought it with plans to turn it into a plush private club. Unfortunately the sheik went bankrupt, and once again the building fell into disrepair. Since then, several other efforts to restore the historic tower to its original grandeur have seen fits and starts, but for the past decade the seventeen-story peach beauty has remained a vacant shell.*

Above left, bottom photo: *Downtown Miami's Dade County Courthouse as the sun sets on the city. Home base for the gray-suit-and-briefcase crowd, the courthouse on Flagler Street was built between 1925 and 1928. At its debut, the twenty-seven-story, neoclassical structure was heralded as the tallest building south of Baltimore, Maryland. In the 1930s, on the building's north side, gallows were erected on occasion to hang convicted criminals. A more humorous aspect of the building's lore is that each fall a flock of migrating turkey vultures commandeer the courthouse roof and turn it into their winter home. Some lawsuit-weary locals claim that it's often hard to distinguish between the vultures outside and the vultures inside.*

Above right: *The Miami-Dade Cultural Center. Designed by renowned architect Philip Johnson, this bustling downtown center has a beautiful tiled courtyard, a series of granite fountains, and an Italian-style piazza. The structure contains the Historical Museum of Southern Florida, the Miami-Dade Main Library, and the Miami Art Museum. The Historical Museum has a permanent exhibit covering ten thousand years of south Florida history, including a simulated ride on a 1920s Miami trolley car. Exhibits at the Art Museum vary, and they are often accompanied by concerts and lectures.*

Left: *A Cuban-American shoeshine man makes public his political views. The longest-reigning military leader in Latin America, and the most hated man in Miami, Fidel Castro has had a greater influence on this city than any other figure in modern history. Since his takeover of the island in 1959, about six hundred thousand Cuban refugees have sought exile in Miami-Dade County. And for more than forty years, Castro-bashing has been the favorite activity of many Cuban-Americans who live here, especially the first-generation refugees who still long for the "good old days" in Cuba. Several exile groups in the city still actively plot to oust the bearded dictator, and they are often less than tolerant of those who are not sympathetic to their cause.*

Below: *Bayside Marketplace with the Hard Rock Café on the left and the Bayfront Park Amphitheater on the right. A popular spot for live outdoor music, the amphitheater regularly hosts ethnic festivals, laser light shows, and reggae concerts. Bayfront Park itself is a large expanse of waterfront land that was dredged up from the bottom of Biscayne Bay in the 1920s. The park was redesigned in 1987. At the southern end of the park is a double-helix sculpture designed by Isamu Noguchi and dedicated to the crew of the ill-fated* Challenger *space shuttle. A walkway at the eastern edge of the park is frequently crowded with joggers and strollers who come to watch the sailboats on the bay.*

Crossing paths with the Pink Lady sight-seeing boat. Dozens of sightseeing water tours are available in various locations around Miami and Miami Beach. Some tours are taken aboard historic tall-masted sailing ships, while others are on air-conditioned cruisers. Most include narration. There are also specialty tours that feature dining and dancing, tours of million-dollar mansions on the bay, romantic moonlit tours, murder mystery excursions, and Las Vegas–like gambling boats that travel three miles offshore into international waters where it's legal to open the blackjack tables and start up the slot machines.

A fully loaded cargo ship sets sail from the Port of Miami. Over six million tons of cargo sails out of the Port of Miami every year, carried by shipping lines serving almost every port in the world. More than 40 percent of all U.S. exports to South America, Central America, and the Caribbean pass through the U.S. Customs District in Miami, which includes the port.

A tugboat hauls a ship down the Miami River. Dissected by many bridges, the Miami River is a working waterway that stretches for over five miles through the city and suburbs. The river is one of the busiest waterways in south Florida. A Seminole trading post once stood along its banks, but today the river is lined with gritty boatyards, marinas, and shipping offices.

Above left: *Two American Airlines jets await takeoff from Miami International Airport (MIA). MIA is the primary connecting point for air travel between the United States and South America and the Caribbean and handles over fifteen hundred flights each day. The twelfth busiest airport in the world, it hosts over one hundred scheduled carriers and forty charter airlines, and sees a total of about thirty-five million passengers per year. About six miles west of downtown and twelve miles from Miami Beach, MIA is a city itself that employs over thirty thousand people. It is equipped with moving sidewalks, an observation/sun deck, DEA-trained drug-sniffing dogs, a prayer chapel, and an Art-in-Public-Places stained-glass exhibit enhanced with the sounds of chirping birds and croaking frogs. Tourists, however, are not impressed with the state of its facilities and services. Recent studies of passenger comment cards reveal that the airport is overcrowded, inefficient, confusing, and lacking sufficient numbers of tourist information booths, parking spaces, and English-speaking employees. More and more tourists are bypassing MIA entirely and flying into the more user-friendly Fort Lauderdale/Hollywood International Airport about twenty miles north of Miami.*

Above right: *Once airborne, this seventeen-passenger Grumman Mallard, shown here taking off from Watson Island, offers a bird's-eye view of Miami. Founded in 1919, this fleet of squat seaplanes, formerly known as Chalks International Airlines and now called the Pan Am Air Bridge, has been flying from Miami to the Bahamas and Key West for decades. During the 1930s, the planes were a favorite means of transportation for Ernest Hemingway. In addition to the regularly scheduled flights, the airline offers low-flying tours of the city.*

Weathered lobster traps stacked alongside the Miami River. Florida lobsters (also known as spiny lobsters) are a smaller version of the northern variety minus the claws. They are called spiny because of the sharp, barb-covered carapace that encases them. Florida lobsters are still found in the waters off Miami and are abundant in the Florida Keys. When fully mature, they can weigh up to fifteen pounds, but the average is one to two pounds. Even though diehard New England lobster lovers often look down upon the southern variety because they dry out easily and can become tough if overcooked, Florida lobsters have a wide tail full of sweet and tender meat and are much easier to shell than northern lobsters.

A Cuban coffee break for boat workers on the Miami River. Served up sweet and swampy, café Cubano is Miami's favorite drink. Brewed in traditional Italian espresso machines, each cup is individually prepared from three scoops of freshly ground Latin American coffee beans and one ounce of scalding-hot water. The beans used to make café Cubano are roasted at a slightly higher temperature and for a longer time than beans used for regular coffee. After the molasses-thick liquid is brewed, two teaspoons of sugar are stirred in. Usually served in thimble-sized pill cups, as shown here, café Cubano became prevalent in Miami in the 1960s after the first wave of Cuban immigrants landed in the city. Unlike the cold weather practice of lingering over a large mug of hot coffee, sipping these tiny, concentrated shots is a sensible way to take coffee in a hot climate. The liquid idiosyncrasy provides a quick caffeine and sugar rush. It is commonly served in nearly every type of business in the city from fancy restaurants to funeral homes, barber shops, and beauty parlors. Although the drink is occasionally served with warm milk in a regular-sized cup, putting milk in true café Cubano is a sacrilege, a social faux pas.

Above: *A stray cat scratches in the sun. The furry vagabonds are the focus of a constant battle that takes place throughout Miami between animal rights activists and those who would rather see the little critters captured and put to sleep. The controversy made headlines in 1999 when music students studying at the New World Symphony complained to school officials about being bitten by fleas from the stray cats that lived on the property. In response, school administrators planned to have the cats captured and taken to local animal shelters, where they would likely be put to sleep. But Cat Network, a local volunteer group, came to the rescue and organized a peaceful truce, under which the cats were taken to no-kill shelters.*

Right, top: *The Metromover is an elevated electric train that loops through four and one-half miles (7 km) of downtown Miami and offers one of the best and cheapest (twenty-five cents) tours of the area. Also known as the People Mover, this little loop connects with the Metrorail system that runs twenty-one miles (33.5 km) from the Dadeland Mall in the southwestern Kendall neighborhood north to the city of Hialeah. Often called Metro Fail by locals, the system cost a bundle to build but never lived up to expectations. It remains underused and does not connect to the neighborhoods in Miami-Dade County that most need public transportation.*

Right, bottom: *The hot-off-the-press* Miami Herald *reports on the status of the Miami Circle, an ancient Tequesta Indian site discovered in the heart of downtown Miami. The most widely read local paper in Florida, the* Herald *(with editions in English and Spanish) is the only major newspaper in Miami. Although its circulation has dwindled in recent years, it is still home to several Pulitzer prize–winning writers, including syndicated funny man Dave Barry.*

Above: *The Claude and Mildred Pepper Fountain, named after the late Florida congress-man and his wife, at Bayfront Park. Not far from the fountain is a bronze marker that commemorates the place where an unemployed bricklayer named Giuseppe Zangara tried to assassinate President-elect Franklin D. Roosevelt in 1933. Roosevelt had just finished speaking to a crowd at the park when Zangara began firing a .32-caliber pistol. He missed Roosevelt, but mortally wounded Anton Cermak, the mayor of Chicago.*

Right: *Often remembered from the opening sequence of the television series* Miami Vice, *the twenty-one-story Atlantis condominium on Brickell Avenue is a haughty exclamation point from the flamboyant local architectural firm Arquitectonica. It is said that the design for the building was originally drawn on a table napkin at a Cuban restaurant in the city. Usually referred to as the "building with the hole in it," Atlantis's twelfth-floor cut-out center cube called the "skycourt" is a surreal space marked by a red circular staircase, a freeform Jacuzzi, and a lonely palm tree. An identically sized cube of concrete sits on the ground below the "skycourt" and appears as if it was knocked out and fell there—pure illusion. Director Brian De Palma filmed a portion of* Scarface, *his movie about cocaine cowboys, at the Atlantis.*

Facing page: *Arguably the most distinctive building in the downtown skyline, the NationsBank Tower has a less than sterling history. Designed by architect I. M. Pei, the forty-seven-story local landmark was originally constructed as the headquarters of the now-failed CenTrust Bank by David Paul, CenTrust's chairman. After a long and tumul-tuous financial scandal, federal banking regulators seized the building and threw Paul in jail for bank fraud. Along with gold-leaf ceilings and marble floors, the building has an elaborate lighting system that enables the exterior colors to fit the mood of the day—blue with snowflakes on Christmas, aqua and orange when the Miami Dolphins have an impor-tant game, emerald green on St. Patrick's Day.*

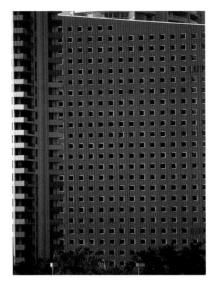

"There was only one job in the world I would have traded my own for, and that was the one in Miami. It was a reporter's nirvana . . . "
—Rick Bragg, New York *Times* reporter and author, *All Over but the Shoutin'*, 1997

Top, left: *The multi-hued Villa Regina and the Palace Condominium. Designed by Arquitectonica in the 1980s for real estate mogul Harry Helmsley, owner of the Empire State Building in New York City, the Palace was originally called the Helmsley Palace. When Helmsley's wife Leona saw the plans for the $30 million condominium she allegedly said, "Honey, the kids have done their homework. I like it." After Leona landed in jail, the name Helmsley was dropped from the building.*

Top, right: *Although constructed to withstand hurricane-force winds, many downtown skyscrapers would not fare well if they took a direct hit from a major storm. After Hurricane Andrew wiped out much of southern Miami-Dade County in 1992, downtown real estate developers realized that their towering structures full of plate-glass windows are beautiful to look at, but would likely shatter and crumble if a hurricane were to hit. Since Hurricane Andrew, the county's building codes have become more stringent, and consequently, the cost of construction has risen.*

Right: *The Intercontinental Bank in downtown Miami. With the largest concentration of banks on the East Coast south of New York, Miami has become the banking capital of Latin America. Together, Miami-Dade County's fifty-six commercial banks bring in over $26 billion in deposits each year. In addition, an estimated five hundred multinational corporations now operate in Miami-Dade County, with more than 40 percent of these having established offices here in the past decade.*

Miami youth. Once a city full of retirees, Miami's demographics have seen drastic changes in the past decade. With the recent influx of immigrants—mostly people under forty—Miami-Dade County's population of citizens over age sixty-five is now only 15 percent. As a result, the proportion of the local population aged twenty-five to forty-four is higher than it is for the entire state of Florida, and the immigrant infusion is seen as a fountain of youth for the city.

A boy and his dad out for an afternoon boat ride. The generational gap is wide between immigrants and their native-born children. Although most children of Hispanic immigrants in Miami are bilingual in Spanish and English, many communicate in what is called "Spanglish," a mixture of the two languages. Some wind up not being fluent in either language, especially when it comes to reading and writing. And since a large group of Hispanic immigrants in Miami never learn to speak English, particularly Cuban immigrants who believe they will one day return to Cuba, some children serve as translators for their parents, grandparents, aunts, and uncles.

The University of Miami Hurricanes play ball at the Orange Bowl Stadium near downtown Miami. Since the 1980s, the Hurricanes, a Big East team, have consistently been ranked one of the best teams in the league and have captured four national championships. Their games are often more exciting to watch than those of the NFL's Miami Dolphins. Spread out over 260 lush acres (100 ha) in the city of Coral Gables, the University of Miami has worked diligently in the past ten years to change its frivolous reputation as Suntan-U by strengthening its law school, medical school, and college of arts and sciences. Opened in 1926, the school today has about 14,000 students and is the second-largest private employer in Miami-Dade County with over 8,200 employees, slightly fewer than American Airlines, which employs more than 9,000.

Above: *One of the oldest Catholic parishes in Miami, the Gesu Catholic Church is a peaceful respite from the bustle of downtown. The Mediterranean-revival structure, built in the mid-1920s, has an ornate mural painted on the ceiling that a Nicaraguan refugee completely restored in the late 1980s.*

Right: *The Big Fish before the music starts. Right on the Miami River near downtown, the Big Fish is well known for its quirky atmosphere, waterfront view, and Latin-style fresh seafood. But for in-the-know locals, the Big Fish is also the best place in Miami to catch some live Afro-Brazilian music. Every weekend, the hypnotic and sensual sound of music direct from the interior of Brazil is performed, and the Big Fish really comes alive.*

Above: *With its plush, red velvet seats, the Gusman Center for the Performing Arts was built for Paramount Pictures in the mid-1920s as an ornate and romantic Spanish-style movie theater, complete with billowing clouds and twinkling stars painted on the ceiling. Although it has come close to extinction several times in the past ten years, the Gusman manages to find a benefactor every time it's threatened with financial doom—once, actor Sylvester Stallone came to the rescue with the needed funds. Today, it hosts dance, theater, and musical events, and each February is one of the main venues for the Miami International Film Festival.*

Left: *The sixty-five-foot (20-meter) revolving electric guitar of Hard Rock Café juts into the sky at Bayside Marketplace. Founded in London in 1971, the Fortune 500 chain of burger joints/rock-and-roll shrines added Miami to its roster of cities in 1993. In addition to the chain's standard gold records, autographs, concert ticket stubs, and rock star guitars, Miami's Hard Rock Café has a definite Latin music slant with memorabilia from local music celebrities Gloria Estefan and John Secada.*

"I don't know why anyone who could live in Miami would choose to live in New York City. This place is a million times better without all the hassle."
—Antonio Lopez, advertising salesman

A Sensual Oasis

"Something about our sultry summers and their madness energizes me. I need less sleep, and I wake earlier from technicolor dreams to greet spectacular dawns with no need of an alarm clock."
—Edna Buchanan, author

Above: *The color green is ever present throughout Miami, especially at Fairchild Tropical Garden where this frond was photographed. Fairchild Garden, in the city of Coral Gables, is an eighty-three-acre (33-hectare) Garden of Eden. Created in 1938 and named in honor of botanist and explorer David Fairchild, known as the Christopher Columbus of American horticulture, Fairchild Garden is one of the most acclaimed tropical gardens in the Western Hemisphere. It contains about 700 species of palms, 150 species of cycads (ancient and endangered palmlike plants), more than 5,000 species of rare and exotic plants, a 7,000-volume library, and a 65,000-sheet herbarium where valuable research slides are housed. About 25 percent of the world's prescription drugs come from plants, and Fairchild Garden's specimens have been used in the search for cures for cancer and the HIV virus. It is also a beautiful and magical place where vibrant elephant ears glisten in the sun and Queen of Sheba vines reach toward the sky. And on breezy days, the sweet scent of ylang-ylang blossoms—one of the prime ingredients in Chanel No. 5 perfume—wafts through the air.*

Facing page: *A bicyclist rides into the sunset on the Rickenbacker Causeway from Key Biscayne. So flat is Miami that serious cyclists in training for marathons or cross-country trips have only the arched bridges and causeways of the city to gain experience riding up hills. Miami-Dade County has about one hundred miles (160 km) of paved bicycle paths, many of which meander through dense foliage and past beautiful old homes. There are also several bicycle clubs in the area, and early on Saturday and Sunday mornings packs of single-file cyclists whir through sleepy neighborhoods.*

Right, top: *The European-style gardens leading to the entranceway of the Doral Golf Resort and Spa. Rated as one of the best spas in Florida, the Doral focuses on physical fitness as well as spiritual well-being, and combines ancient health traditions with modern techniques. The spa's tranquil landscape has a meditative, Zen-like atmosphere that inspires guests to slow down, relax, and reflect.*

Right, bottom: *A waterfront view of Vizcaya Museum and Gardens. Designed to resemble an Italian country villa and to appear as if it were three hundred years old, Vizcaya is one of the most beautiful attractions in Miami. Each March it hosts an Italian Renaissance Festival with drama productions, fortunetellers, court jesters, a life-size chessboard that uses people for pieces, and a food buffet that features wild boar. Original pilings, dug deep into the ground, saved the villa from collapse during the 1926 hurricane, and during Hurricane Andrew in 1992 it sustained only minor damage. Miami-Dade County purchased Vizcaya in 1952, turning it into a museum for the public, which now attracts over 250,000 visitors a year.*

Facing page: *An interior room of Villa Vizcaya. The seventy rooms of Vizcaya are maintained in original condition, complete with millions of dollars worth of European furnishings, art, antiques, musical instruments, fine china, silverware, tapestries, and Oriental rugs. The interior combines Renaissance, baroque, rococo, and neoclassical styles. Ground-floor rooms are arranged around a central courtyard and include a reception area, banquet hall, tearoom, music room, smoking room, and library. Sleeping quarters are on the second floor. The basement, a rarity in Florida, holds the service areas that were always kept out of view from the many well-to-do guests who came for the winter.*

A totem pole at the Miccosukee Indian Village within the Miccosukee Indian Reservation near Everglades National Park. About thirty miles west of downtown Miami, the village offers visitors a glimpse of a disappearing culture. The Miccosukee were originally part of the Creek Nation, an association of Indian clans in the areas now known as the states of Alabama and Georgia. The Miccosukee belonged to the lower Creek region, and in the 1700s the Spaniards relocated them to Florida land already occupied by the Seminole tribe. Eventually, the Miccosukee branched off from the Seminole, and the Miccosukee were officially recognized by the U.S. government in 1962 as a Native American tribe. Their community has about five hundred members and its own clinic, police department, court system, seniors program, daycare center, and school. The Miccosukee Indian Village is open to the public and features huts known as chickees, which have thatched roofs made of palm branches; traditional arts and crafts; patchwork clothing; alligator wrestling demonstrations; airboat rides; basket weaving; wood carving; and native foods, such as alligator tail, fried catfish, wild boar, frog legs, and fry bread. Not far from the village is the newly opened Miccosukee Resort and Convention Center, a $55 million gaming hall that offers high-stakes gambling and big-name entertainment. Like other Native American tribes across the United States, the Miccosukee function as a sovereign nation, with their own constitution and bylaws, and are therefore immune to prosecution under Florida's anti-gambling laws.

Above: *A lone white ibis takes flight. One of the more common wading birds of south Florida and the official mascot of the University of Miami, the white ibis is frequently found in salt marshes, lakes, and other wetlands. Their favorite foods are crab, shrimp, crayfish, insects, and small fish. Usually about two feet (60 cm) tall when fully mature, many of them head north for the summer, some going as far away as the Great Lakes. They often fly in huge flocks in a typical V formation or straight line, and these formations may extend for over a mile (1.6 km) in length. Although they are not an endangered species, their numbers are declining because encroaching development is eating away at the natural wetlands, where they prefer to nest.*

Left: *In the southern part of Miami-Dade County, Orchid Jungle, which featured glorious orchids such as this, was once a lush oasis in the middle of a natural hammock where rare and exotic orchids from around the world were cultivated year-round. Unfortunately, in 1992 Hurricane Andrew wiped out most of Orchid Jungle's foliage, and the attraction has yet to be rebuilt. Orchid growing is, however, a favorite hobby of many Miami residents, and the delicate flowers can be found at almost all nurseries and plant shops in the area with price tags as outrageous as their colors.*

Left, top: *She sells seashells by the seashore. While it's the southwest coast of Florida that is really known as a shell-collector's haven, Miami's beaches do indeed toss up waterfront treasures, with the best pickings right after a coastal storm (but not after a more violent hurricane) or during low tide. The most commonly found shells are the prickly cockle, yellow cockle, calico scallop, bay scallop, eastern oyster, quahog, and banded tulip. Forget about finding a large pink-and-white beauty of a queen conch shell, since the queen conch is a protected species that has all but disappeared from Miami's shores. Queen conchs are, however, imported from the Caribbean and sold in many gift shops.*

Left, bottom: *A swimmer glides through the Venetian Pool. Carved out of an old coral rock quarry, the Venetian Pool in Coral Gables was built in the 1920s as an entertainment center that hosted beauty pageants, gondola rides, aquatic shows, moonlit dancing, and live orchestras. Called the most beautiful swimming hole in the world and listed on the National Register of Historic Landmarks, the Venetian Pool is actually a free-form, freshwater lagoon complete with caves, waterfalls, stone bridges, Spanish porticos, fountains, and lush landscaping. Its Venetian-style architecture and soft, sandy beach draw hundreds of locals and tourists daily. Since the eight-hundred-thousand-gallon (three-million-liter) pool is emptied every night and refilled early every morning with water from an underground artesian well, a swim here is surprisingly cool.*

Facing page: *A brown-spotted, yellow-wing dragonfly, also known as a Halloween pennant, makes a graceful landing. Common in Miami from mid-April onward, this species frequents the edges of ponds with weedy bottoms. Since dragonfly larvae develop in warm water, Miami is often full of the insects. Over 120 different types of dragonflies are said to make Florida their home. Other insects abundant in Miami are butterflies, moths, grasshoppers, crickets, fireflies, fire ants, palmetto bugs, beetles, scorpions, silk spiders, caterpillars, water bugs, love bugs, palm weevils, and the dreaded, far-too-abundant mosquito.*

"In Miami the seasons shift not by changes in foliage or in temperature, but by dramatic modulation in the color of the light. In its clear, dry winters, Miami is bathed in a light as golden as that of the south of France."
—Laura Cerwinske, *Miami Hot & Cool,* 1990

Left, top: *A young woman enjoys the rush of refreshing water at the Doral Golf Resort and Spa. Located, surprisingly, in an industrial area just west of the Miami International Airport, the Doral is Miami's largest resort property. Its full-service, award-winning spa features massage, aromatherapy, yoga, saunas, mud wraps, sea salt scrubs, tap dancing, aqua-aerobics, stress therapy, astrological readings, hydrotherapy, and an assortment of other healthful pleasures.*

Left, center: *A pocket of green on Granada Boulevard in Coral Gables. Miami-Dade County has a total of 696 parks and recreation areas totaling 1.05 million acres (420,000 ha) including Biscayne National Park and about half of Everglades National Park.*

Left, bottom: *The underwater mosaic that is John Pennekamp Coral Reef State Park. A ninety-minute drive south of Miami, in the upper Florida Keys, Pennekamp is the most visited state park in Florida, receiving over two million tourists a year. Covering about one hundred square miles (160 sq. km), the park is a haven for some 650 species of fish amid a fragile ecosystem that includes fifty-five varieties of coral. Along with hosting an array of plant life such as lavender sea fans, sponges, sea cucumbers, and sea fingers, the reef serves as an underwater condominium of sorts for parrot fish, grouper, snapper, crabs, lobsters, barracuda, and sharks. Whether viewed with scuba gear, snorkel and mask, or by glass-bottom boat, the park's underwater scenery is nothing less than spectacular.*

Facing page: *With its outstretched arms and somber face, the Christ of the Deep statue is an eerie sight to behold. Twenty feet (6 m) under water, near Key Largo Dry Rocks reef inside John Pennekamp Coral Reef State Park, the nine-foot bronze (2.75-meter) sculpture is a replica of the Christ of the Abyss statue off the coast of Genoa, Italy. Donated by an Italian industrialist and sport fisherman, the statue is one of the most popular dive sites in Florida. Every now and then park rangers are sent out to scrape off the green algae that continuously forms on the statue.*

Above: *The oceanfront Sheraton Bal Harbour Beach Resort. The town of Bal Harbour, at the northern tip of Miami Beach, is a pricey community with one of the highest per capita incomes in the state. It's full of high-rise condominiums and includes the fifteen-acre (6-hectare) promenade known as the Bal Harbour Shops where Gucci, Fendi, and Tiffany's are the boutiques of choice. Once a winter retreat for the old-money crowd, Bal Harbour has recently begun to attract young families with children, and its once-rigid social structure is a thing of the past.*

Facing page: *The lush gardens and waterfalls of the Sheraton Bal Harbour Beach Resort. It's not just fancy hotels that have landscaping and pools as exotic as this in Miami. Many private homes in Coral Gables, Coconut Grove, and Key Biscayne in particular have their own hidden oasis in the back yard, equipped with swimming pools, grottos, waterfalls, fish ponds, sun decks, outdoor showers, orchid gardens, aviaries, and hot tubs big enough to comfortably seat six people.*

A peaceful sunrise on the beach. Although skies here are usually calm and clear, Miami has indeed seen its share of brutal hurricanes, and during hurricane season (June through October) residents are often nervous when a storm is brewing in the nearby Caribbean. In 1926, a killer storm that left more than 100 people dead ravaged the young city. And in 1992, Hurricane Andrew killed 40 people, left 160,000 homeless, and caused more than $25 billion damage in Florida and in Louisiana, where it made a second landfall. Packing 160-mph winds, Andrew slammed into the southern tier of Miami-Dade County just before dawn on August 24. Hardest hit were the rural and suburban areas about twenty miles (32 km) south of downtown Miami. Along with leaving demolished buildings, smashed cars, overturned boats, and debris for miles, Andrew uprooted one-hundred-year-old trees and severely scarred the natural landscape. In the weeks and months that followed, thousands of civilian volunteers from around the country, along with over twenty thousand U.S. troops, came to Miami to help rebuild entire communities. The U.S. soldiers, many of whom had just returned from war-torn areas of Kuwait, said that they had never seen such massive destruction in all their lives.

"Every day, as I sit on the beach looking out at the ocean, each
palm tree, each wave, each sea gull is still a revelation to me.
After all these years, Miami Beach feels like home."
—the late Isaac Bashevis Singer, author and Nobel laureate

Above: *A banyan tree canopy in Coral Gables. A relative of the mulberry tree, banyans are very common in Miami. Although they look beautiful and provide shade with their thick foliage, which is practical in a hot and sunny place like Miami, they can be a nuisance. Their branches send out shoots that drop to the ground and then root in the soil to form secondary trunks. By doing this, they often cause problems for sewer systems and sidewalks.*

Right: *Stalks of freshly cut sugar cane await being turned into guarapo. A favorite Latin American drink, guarapo (pronounced wa-RA-po) is made by feeding the sugar cane stalks into an industrial strength juicer. The light green liquid, only mildly sweet, has an earthy plantlike flavor that hints of alfalfa sprouts. In addition to being served over ice as a refreshing drink, guarapo is used in rum cocktails and boiled down to make a thick, sweet syrup.*

Far right: *Blame it on the mango. In the early 1980s, Miami made it onto culinary maps because of a group of local chefs who were doing some very strange things with mangos. Allen Susser, Norman Van Aken, and Douglas Rodriguez combined the sweet and exotic locally grown fruit with all sorts of other ingredients—fish, chicken, meats, vegetables—and voilà, New World Cuisine was born. Also called Floribbean and Tropical Fusion, this new Cuisine combined classic European techniques, fresh tropical ingredients, and a liberal dash of Caribbean and Latin flavorings. The chefs were nicknamed the Mango Gang, and their creations made waves not just in Miami, but across the country. Since New World cuisine dishes are low in fat and high in flavor, the cooking style caught on quickly, especially with health-conscious gourmets.*

"As long as you don't have to spend the hot summer here, Miami is wonderful. July and August, whew, are they rough."
—Samuel Kaufman, Boston-born stockbroker

Rows of herbs are cultivated in the farming communities of the Redland and Homestead, about twenty-five miles (40 km) south of Miami. Still surprisingly peaceful and rural, these areas are full of rich farmland that also produces strawberries, tomatoes, beans, squash, limes, oranges, mangos, star fruit, passion fruit, mameys, lychees, and avocados.

Throughout Miami, heaping piles of black beans are a common sight at corner grocery stores. Black beans and rice, also called moros y cristianos, *are a Miami dinnertime staple that can be traced back to Spain by way of Cuba. Usually simmered with onions, bay leaf, and garlic, black beans are spooned over fluffy white rice to accompany chicken, fish, or beef dishes. Cuban chefs say the secret to keeping the beans' black color is to cook them in the same water that they were soaked in, instead of discarding it and starting fresh. The beans are also made into a hearty soup, combined with tomatoes and peppers to make a cold salad, and mashed and transformed into a refried pancake.*

The interior courtyard of the Biltmore Hotel in Coral Gables. Dining al fresco is a fact of life in Miami, and it doesn't just take place in hotels and restaurants. Most single-family homes have an outdoor area set aside specifically for dining. Some are screened in to protect from mosquitoes, but most are wide open to the elements. Even most apartments and condominiums come with private balconies to insure at least some regular contact with Mother Nature. Dinner napkins blow away with the wind, leaves fall on the table, and an occasional rain shower causes a commotion. But in the end, it's all worth it.

One of the oldest tourist attractions in south Florida, Parrot Jungle in southern Miami is a venerable institution in which hundreds of rare parrots fly free. In the nearby neighborhoods, residents are often greeted early in the morning with the squawk of these loud creatures; each morning about fifty macaws are released to fly around the city, and they return—voluntarily—every night. Visitors can wander through Parrot Jungle's twelve-acre (5-hectare) exotic garden where showy peacocks strut and flamingos wade in the water, or pose for a silly souvenir photo with a half-dozen macaws perched on their arms. In addition to the must-see roller-skating cockatoos, Parrot Jungle also has a petting zoo, and iguanas, alligators, and tortoises on display.

Above: *The pink flamingos that live in a protected bird sanctuary designated by the National Audubon Society at Hialeah Race Track. Originally imported from Cuba, the eight hundred or so birds that permanently reside here make up the only reproducing flamingo colony in North America. Almost synonymous with Florida, this wading bird, officially called* Phoenicopterus ruber *or the American flamingo, prefers to feed in shallow salt water by sweeping its head back and forth to sift for crustaceans. Aside from those found at Hialeah and other tourist attractions, flocks of wild flamingos are a common site in Miami, especially in the winter months. In the racetrack's gift shop, and at many other tacky souvenir shops in Miami, plastic lawn flamingos are a popular item.*

Right: *The wooden walkway that leads to Cape Florida beach on Key Biscayne. This four-hundred-acre (160-hectare) playground is regularly listed on Florida International University marine research scientist Stephen Leatherman's much-heralded Twenty Best Beaches in America list. Officially known as Bill Baggs Cape Florida State Recreation Area, the park is named after a local newspaper editor who led a crusade to preserve this piece of land. At the southern end of Key Biscayne, it's a glorious spread of soft sand dunes dotted with sea grapes and sea oats. Not at all commercial, it looks like a pristine beach in the out islands of the Bahamas and is home to a robust population of raccoons and rabbits. The historic, red-brick Cape Florida Lighthouse, built in the 1820s to help sailors find their way to shore, is at the farthest end of the beach.*

Facing page: *A sailboat drops anchor offshore. Each fall, the waters off Miami teem with sailboats competing in the annual Columbus Day Regatta. A two-day event that takes sailors from Coconut Grove to Elliott Key in Biscayne National Park and back, the regatta is legendary in the city not for the six hundred or so boats that compete, or the two thousand or so boaters who anchor offshore to watch, but for the abundance of topless women and bottomless men who traditionally grace the bows of the racing crafts. A local tradition since the 1950s, the race includes sailboats of all types and sizes, and is also noted for the uninhibited bacchanalia that it always manages to set in motion on land.*

The Deco Lifestyle

"The great thing about Miami is that you can work your butt off, make money, and then go outside and feel like you're on vacation."
—Joe Rubin, businessman

Above: *Reading at the beach. A thriving literary community is not what first comes to mind when people think of Miami. But the area is indeed full of writers. Among the authors that call the Miami area home, even if only on a part-time basis, are Dave Barry, Edna Buchanan, Carl Hiaasen, Les Standiford, Anne Rice, Dan Wakefield, Charles Willeford, Christine Bell, and Edward Albee. And each November, downtown Miami hosts the annual Miami International Book Fair, a ten-day literary event that brings together about one hundred authors and over five hundred thousand readers.*

Facing page: *A typical stretch of Ocean Drive. The pastel cityscape of Miami Beach's Art Deco District has come to represent the golden egg of the area's tourism industry. Ever since* Miami Vice *first projected the seductive scenes of pale blues and pretty pinks to television viewers around the world in 1984, these images have been synonymous with Miami Beach.*

Above: *The shifting sands of time. The city of Miami Beach has spent millions of dollars in a constant battle against beach erosion on its seven-mile-long (11-kilometer-long) oceanfront. With the help of the U.S. Army Corps of Engineers, the city of has piled tons of fine white sand—some dredged and sucked up from the ocean floor and some shipped over from the nearby Bahama Islands— on Miami Beach to build and maintain what has become a world-famous shoreline.*

Right: *Young boys heading home from the beach. The tall, white building on the left with the spire on top is the Loews Miami Beach Hotel. Opened in 1998, the Loews is the first new hotel built on South Beach in over thirty years. Just four blocks from the Miami Beach Convention Center, the 738-room property has made attending a convention on the beach much easier and more convenient.*

Left: *A sand castle under construction. Not taken lightly by those who do it, sand castle building is actually a profession for a few lucky people. Along with competing in tournaments that offer substantial prize money, some sand castle designers are hired by hotels to entertain guests and teach their skills.*

Above: *Authentic Art Deco details. Between World War I and World War II, over five hundred Art Deco structures were built in the southern part of Miami Beach. Intentionally designed to lift the spirits of war-weary Americans, the buildings indeed provided a needed fantasy escape. During World War II, tourists flocked to Miami Beach's Art Deco hotels to listen to big band sounds and dance under a full moon. Common themes in Miami Beach's Art Deco style and the Art Moderne style that followed include rounded corners, geometric forms, racing stripes, glass blocks, etched glass panels, pastel colors, porthole windows, overhanging canopies called eyebrows, and decorative murals of mermaids, nymphs, flowers, flamingos, pelicans, and sea horses. During the 1950s, the Art Deco hotels continued to prosper, but in the 1960s they began to decay, and by the 1970s they rapidly declined as paint cracked and walls crumbled. In 1976 the Miami Design Preservation League was created to stop the demolition of these decrepit structures and to encourage their restoration. Soon after, hotel owners, historians, civic leaders, and residents jumped on the bandwagon to add their support. In 1979, what is now called the Art Deco District was placed on the National Register of Historic Places, the first collection of twentieth-century structures to be granted such a distinction. Today, the district represents the largest concentration of Art Deco architecture in the world.*

Right: *Barstools await thirsty patrons. While most bars and restaurants in South Beach welcome customers in casual clothing—shorts, jeans, sandals, tank tops—there are a few velvet-rope establishments with dress codes that determine whether or not you get in the door. For these hot-ticket clubs with an attitude, wearing black is always desirable and looking like a model is even better.*

A tourist takes in some sun. Every year, about ten million domestic and international tourists visit the Miami area. The largest numbers of foreign tourists come from Canada, Brazil, Germany, Venezuela, Colombia, Argentina, England, France, Italy, and Peru. The highest number of domestic visitors come from New York, Philadelphia, Chicago, Atlanta, Boston, and Washington D.C.

Haydee and Sahara Scull, Cuban-born artists, live and work in Miami Beach. Easily recognizable by their flamboyant matching clothing and less-than-modest makeup, the twins are a vivacious fixture of the local landscape. Their highly praised folk art—colorful three-dimensional collages and figurines—depicts scenes from their pre-Castro life in Havana and is featured at several Miami Beach restaurants. "We can never be separate," Haydee once told an interviewer. "Together makes us strong. Four arms. Four legs. One heart. One mind. One soul."

Wall art and body art at a South Beach café. Murals like the one in this photograph are abundant throughout Miami. Some are created by well-known artists, others are produced by struggling, upstart art students.

Condos, condos, and more condos. At least that's what longtime residents of Miami say they see popping up all around them. Trying to find the right balance between allowing more modern development while also sustaining a livable community is one of the difficult challenges facing many Miami neighborhoods today. Meanwhile, not many locals welcome the "mini-Manhattan" look of the new high-rise condominiums that often cost upwards of one hundred thousand dollars for a tiny studio apartment.

Housed in a restored 1936 Orthodox synagogue in an area of Miami Beach once known for its brazen "No Jews Allowed" signs, the Sanford L. Ziff Jewish Museum is dedicated to explaining the history of Jews in Florida dating back to the first arrivals over 230 years ago. Included in its permanent exhibit are antique menorahs, silver samovars and goblets, historic photos, immigration documents, and Judaic memorabilia, as well as a small collection of artifacts depicting the lives of Jews in Cuba until 1959, when many emigrated to Miami Beach following Fidel Castro's takeover of the island.

The body beautiful is always on display in Miami. Parading around in various states of undress is common, vanity and hedonism are acceptable, and showing off is considered a birthright. Liposuction and tummy tucks are big business here, as are facelifts, acid skin peels, hair transplants, and nose jobs. While the rest of the country lathers on sun block even on cloudy days, many Miamians still worship the sun and work quite hard at maintaining a bronzed glow, oblivious to the fact that Florida has one of the highest skin cancer rates in the United States.

Chin-ups at the beach. About a dozen of Miami's beaches and public parks offer vita courses for an outdoor workout. A series of walking/jogging paths with designated stops for chin-ups, sit-ups, and other body-building exercises, Miami's vita courses are popular playgrounds for health-conscious adults and youngsters.

A salesclerk awaits customers on Miami Beach. A favorite diversion for both locals and tourists, shopping is big business for the local economy. According to the Miami Herald, the retail industry employs over four hundred thousand people in south Florida.

55

Lincoln Road, a pedestrian-only thorough-fare on South Beach. Located between Six-teenth and Seventeenth Streets in the heart of the Art Deco District, the Road, as it is called by locals, is one of the hottest spots in all of south Florida. Once called the Fifth Avenue of the South, the street fell into serious disrepair in the 1970s, but was totally transformed in the 1990s. Now it's full of art galleries, bookstores, clothing boutiques, gourmet restaurants, cafés, the-aters, movie houses, coffee bars, and night-clubs. Every night the street is jam-packed with dog walkers, couples, kids, drag queens, joggers, rollerbladers, and stroll-ing musicians. Every weekend it hosts an outdoor farmers' market, and on the sec-ond Saturday of every month, the local art merchants host a gallery walk.

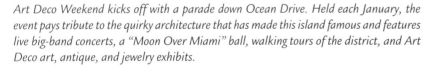

Art Deco Weekend kicks off with a parade down Ocean Drive. Held each January, the event pays tribute to the quirky architecture that has made this island famous and features live big-band concerts, a "Moon Over Miami" ball, walking tours of the district, and Art Deco art, antique, and jewelry exhibits.

Body art at the beach. As over thirty tat-too parlors and piercing salons attest, body art is definitely en vogue in Miami with both men and women. Nose rings, belly-button rings, and tongue rings are also com-mon. Some of the shops offer everything-you-always-wanted-to-know-about-tattoos-but-were-afraid-to-ask seminars and dem-onstrations. Almost all shops are full of in-teresting characters. And for the curious but conservative crowd, temporary, peel-off tattoos are readily available.

Beach cabanas behind the Delano Hotel. For rent by the hour or by the day, beach lounge chairs and umbrellas that provide an escape from the direct sun are available at many beach locations. Not surprisingly, the beach-chair and umbrella-concession booth business is very profitable.

A seaside bike ride on a winter evening—with a classic bike that fits right in with the Art Deco surroundings. Located a few degrees above the Tropic of Cancer, Miami is a subtropical paradise of verdant beauty with an average yearly temperature of a mild seventy-five degrees Fahrenheit (24° C). The change in seasons here is more subtle than in most of the United States. Summers do get hot, with average temperatures around ninety-five degrees Fahrenheit (35° C), but afternoon showers usually cool things off. And the winters are glorious—balmy days, cool nights.

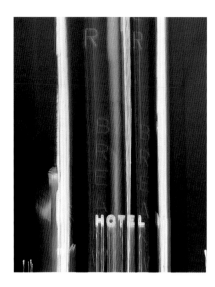

Above: *The Breakwater Hotel's neon rainbow. One of Miami Beach's classic Art Deco buildings, the Breakwater exhibits inset vertical neon stripes that are a common trait of these structures. It was here, on Miami Beach, that neon was first introduced as an integral part of architectural design. Unlike the economical and efficient look of northern Art Deco structures such as New York City's Chrysler Building, Miami Beach's fanciful structures took the vernacular trend and adapted it to fit a tropical setting.*

Right: *Hotels along the Intracoastal Waterway in Miami Beach. At the center of this strip of hotels, marked by a ten-story blue-and-white mural, is the Fontainebleau Hilton Resort and Towers. Designed by flamboyant architect Morris Lapidus in 1954, the Fontainebleau still stands as a tropical symbol of the ostentatious postwar economic boom of the 1950s. A grand dinosaur of a lost era, it has crystal chandeliers, marble floors, and a two-story lagoon pool complete with waterfalls and a floating bar. It was here in the 1950s that the Rat Pack congregated, and if the walls could talk, they would surely tell racy stories of the antics of Frank Sinatra, Sammy Davis Jr., and Dean Martin.*

Above: *Streamline in the tropics—the interior lobby of the St. Moritz Hotel. Sleek and cool building materials are common in Miami Beach hotels. Among the most popular are marble, stucco, mother-of-pearl, limestone, and terrazzo (a cast conglomerate of marble or granite particles in polished and colored cement).*

Right: *Casa Casuarina, the Ocean Drive mansion of the late Italian fashion designer Gianni Versace. Originally built in 1930 and designed as a replica of the Santo Domingo home of Christopher Columbus's son, Diego, the house resembles a sixteenth-century Mediterranean palazzo complete with fifteen-foot-high (4.6-meter) antique wooden doors. During the 1970s and 1980s, the building was known as the Amsterdam Palace and contained dozens of one-bedroom apartments. Versace bought the building for $2.9 million in 1992. Shortly after, he purchased the Revere Hotel next door for $3.7 million and demolished it to make room for gardens and a swimming pool. How much he spent on the renovation was never revealed, but he used the palatial twelve-bedroom home filled with antiques, murals, and mosaics as a vacation spot for his family, and a showplace for his art and design collection. After buying the morning paper at the News Café a few blocks away, Versace was murdered on the front steps of his home in the summer of 1997.*

The News Café on Ocean Drive. Since it opened in 1988, the News Café has been packed with people both day and night. Part restaurant, part jazz club, and part newsstand, it is one of the most popular eateries and people-watching spots on Miami Beach, with a faithful clientele of models and photographers. For such a trendy location, the food is surprisingly good, but not nearly as delightful as the oceanfront view.

Dancing to the South Beach beat. Although most forms of world music can be found in Miami, Latin music and Latin dance clearly dominate the local club scene.

New and improved Art Deco designs at Fifth Street on South Beach. Modern, imitation—Art Deco buildings like this one have been built in recent years trying to capitalize on the trendy South Beach theme. This particular building houses the China Grill restaurant, a New York transplant and posh Pan Asian eatery that's popular with celebrities and celebrity wannabes. Not far from the China Grill is the former site of the Fifth Street Gym, where a young boxer named Cassius Clay Jr. trained before he changed his name and became known throughout the world as Muhammad Ali.

"Miami is the best place. There are so many cultures here. That's why I moved here because it's a small town that's growing by the minute . . . When it comes to music, it's very rich—all sorts of sounds."
—Ricky Martin, Latin pop star and part-time Miami resident, in *Miami Metro* magazine, June 1999

Left: *Aquatic wall art in Miami Beach. Although the original colors of most of Miami Beach's Art Deco structures tended to be pure white accented with trims and details in flamingo pink, turquoise, bright yellow, and mild purples, these days many buildings are being treated to an extra helping of bold primary colors. Some staunch preservationists are not happy with the changes.*

Below: *Evening at the Clevelander Hotel on Ocean Drive. Famous for its poolside neon bar, the Clevelander is not just an Art Deco hotel, but an often-used location for modeling shoots, tourism brochures, and television commercials. It's also a very loud and boisterous meeting place for the nose-ring, purple-hair, Generation X crowd.*

Facing page: *The stark Delano Hotel. Owned by Studio 54 partner Ian Schrager, the Delano is one of the hottest hotels on South Beach. Originally built in 1947, the structure was extensively renovated in the late 1990s and decorated by designer Philippe Starck, who created an eclectic, all-white trademark décor. For a short period, the hotel's Blue Door restaurant was owned and operated by Madonna.*

Latin Nights and Daytime Diversions

"These days, the frenetic stew that is [Miami] is in major boil mode, bubbling over, influencing the nightlife and restaurants in New York, Los Angeles, and plenty of points in between. It's a hot, hot, ethnic mix, heavy on the Carribbean and South American spice."
—Larry Montali, *Esquire* magazine, June 1999

Above: *Billed as the largest New Year's Eve celebration south of New York's Times Square, the nationally televised King Orange Jamboree Parade attracts about one hundred thousand people to downtown Miami each year. Promoted by organizers as good, clean, all-American fun, the parade snakes past cheering crowds for over two miles (3 km) down Biscayne Boulevard. Included each year are high-school marching bands and choirs from across the country, Clydesdale horses, fireworks, huge helium-filled balloons, Miccosukee Indian displays, floats featuring beauty queens and celebrities, and many costumed cartoon characters for kids.*

Facing page: *A flamenco dancer heats up the night. Originally an Andalusian folk dance dating back to seventeenth-century Spain, flamenco is all the rage in Miami these days. There are clubs that specialize in flamenco shows, dancers who perform on the streets, and schools that offer lessons. One local dance troupe, Ballet Flamenco La Rosa, has garnered much acclaim for its unique style that combines flamenco with elements of Afro-Cuban, Middle Eastern, Celtic, and North African dance.*

Tending bar at Mango's Tropical Café on Miami Beach. Recently ranked sixth among the top thirty-five tipping cities in the United States, Miami is not a bad place to earn a living tending bar or waiting on tables. The jobs are plentiful and relatively easy to come by. While the standard for tips is 15 percent, quite a few local barkeeps expect a whopping 20 percent. And since the city receives a large number of European tourists, many restaurants automatically add a 15 percent gratuity to the bill, a common practice in Europe.

A dancer captivates the crowd at Bash, a nightclub on Miami Beach. The nightclub scene in Miami is constantly changing. One minute a particular club is frequented by celebrities—Madonna, Calvin Klein, Jennifer Lopez, Whitney Houston, Robert De Niro, Ricky Martin, Will Smith, Cameron Diaz—and is so popular that you can't get in the front door. The next minute, that same club is no longer en vogue, and the crowds are heading to the newest hot spot in town.

Freshly washed on-the-rocks glasses wait to be filled. From bloody Mary breakfasts to late-night cocktails, Miami is indeed a liquor-loving town. As in the rest of the United States, the martini has become popular again in recent years, but some of the most commonly ordered drinks remain piña coladas, screwdrivers, daiquiris (supposedly first concocted in Cuba and then made famous by Ernest Hemingway), margaritas, sangria, Cuba Librès (rum and coke with a squeeze of lime), and mojitos (a rum, mint, and lime spritzer).

"My musicians, they're working, they're making money, and creatively, they're making Latin music that has an incredible quality. We have every eye all over the world looking toward Miami."
—Emilio Estefan, music producer, husband of Gloria Estefan, in the
Miami Herald, May 24, 1998

Above left: *On Calle Ocho (Eighth Street) in the commercial heart of Little Havana, Café Nostalgia is a romantic little speakeasy where Cubans gather to dance, sip rum, and reminisce about the good old days of pre-Castro Cuba. Black-and-white films of 1950s Havana are projected on a screen over the stage, Cuban memorabilia covers the walls, and impromptu, late-night jam sessions have included performances by Willy Chirino, Ruben Blades, and members of Gloria Estefan's band.*

Above right: *Disco lives! This particular club in Coconut Grove, as well as dozens of others around Miami, still puts out the glittering disco ball and attracts hordes of club crawlers who come to dance till dawn. Disco fever in fact has roots in Miami. The Bee Gees, Miami residents, recorded some of their songs for the soundtrack of* Saturday Night Fever *at North Miami's Criteria Studios. And another disco-era hit,* Shake Your Booty, *was recorded here by KC and the Sunshine Band. Harry "KC" Casey, the lead singer and a Miami native, named his band after the "Sunshine State."*

Left: *Tap Tap, a Haitian restaurant on Fifth Street in Miami Beach, is much more than just a place to taste authentic Haitian cuisine. With walls covered with Haitian art, Tap Tap is a lively gathering spot for writers, artists, photographers, dancers, and musicians. Most weekend nights the restaurant comes alive with Haitian bands, many direct from Port-au-Prince. It also regularly hosts poetry readings and showings of documentary films about the island. In Haiti, a tap-tap is a type of public transportation, often a pick-up truck or a colorfully painted bus.*

Above: *Billed as the biggest Hispanic heritage festival in the United States, the week-long celebration known as Carnivale Miami saves its grandest party for last. Snaking down Little Havana's Eighth Street for a total of twenty-three blocks, Calle Ocho is the blow-out Sunday street party that attracts hundreds of thousands of people from all over the world. Hot, sweaty, wild, and sexy, the party brings live Latin music to over seventy-five stages along with over five hundred food vendors who serve up fajitas, steak-on-a-stick, rice and beans, fried pork, tortillas, and a cauldron of paella so big it's stirred with a wooden oar. The party also features jugglers, clowns, mimes, games, carnival rides, and swaying shoulders and shaking hips. It is the one day when all of Miami's Hispanic communities—Cuban, Colombian, Venezuelan, Dominican, Puerto Rican, Peruvian, Nicaraguan, Chilean, Guatemalan, Honduran, Brazilian—come together as one.*

Left, top: *A shoulder-to-shoulder crowd watches a musical performance at the Calle Ocho festival in Little Havana. The sizzling Latin festival made its way into the* Guinness Book of World Records *on March 13, 1988, when 119,986 sweaty people—holding on to the hips of the person in front of them—formed the world's longest conga line while local superstar Gloria Estefan performed her hit song, "Conga." The record still stands today.*

Left, bottom: *An ice-cream parlor hawks waffle cones. Miami is not a vanilla town. Most ice-cream parlors here feature flavors that are as exotic as the city itself—mango, mamey, coconut, carambola, banana, tangerine, lychee, passion fruit, tamarind, guava, papaya, and sapote.*

Above: *A family-size platter of paella topped with limes. Made with rice, saffron, shrimp, fish, mussels, clams, and sausage, paella is a popular dish at local Spanish restaurants, usually served with an ice-cold pitcher of sangria.*

Right: *The Miami/Bahamas Goombay Festival in Coconut Grove. Among the city's earliest immigrants, Bahamian craftsmen came to Miami to help build the city in the early 1900s. Soon after, many Bahamian merchant shippers and merchant salvagers developed thriving businesses here. Today, the city pays tribute to its vast Bahamian community with this annual festival. One of the largest black heritage festivals in the United States, Goombay takes place each June and features carnival-style parades, the Royal Bahamian Police Marching Band, live music, the clamor of cowbells and washboards, dancing, arts and crafts, and authentic Bahamian foods such as spicy conch fritters and conch salad that vendors like to say "put some zing in your ting." Goombay's joyous "Junkanoo" characters, dressed in colorful crepe-paper costumes, date back to the Bahamian celebrations of the early 1800s when the islands' African slaves were set free and reveled in the streets.*

Right, top: *Satirical, salty, and fun, the King Mango Strut is Miami's anti-parade parade. Founded in 1982 by local teacher/ artist/lawyer Glen Terry, the Strut came about when Terry's Mango Marching Band, playing kazoos and conch shells, was rejected by the King Orange Jamboree Parade organizers. Now held each December in Coconut Grove, the ever-popular, sometimes controversial Strut has become a local institution that takes pride in bad taste and proves that Miamians have a sense of humor. Along with poking fun at notorious political figures, both local and national, it features cynical spoofs on current events that are chock-full of black humor. In 1998, a bevy of big-haired "Marching Monicas" danced to a new version of* Devil in a Blue Dress.

Right, bottom: *It seems as though more and more Miamians are adopting slithery reptiles, like this lovely lady and her treasured pet. Often, Miamians are seen taking their venom-free friends for a stroll on Miami Beach much to the chagrin of fearful onlookers. And occasionally the Miami Museum of Science and Space Transit Planetarium hosts a "Snake Day" as part of its informative reptile appreciation series; snake owners, accompanied by their pets, are admitted for free.*

"South Beach is one of the few places in America where a man with a beard can walk down the street wearing high heels and an evening gown and nobody even notices."
—Juan Dominguez, waiter

The International Tennis Center on Key Biscayne. Each spring, about one hundred top-rated professional tennis players converge on Key Biscayne for the ten-day Lipton International Players Championship to compete for millions of dollars in cash prizes. Along with hundreds of tennis courts located at hotels and private homes, the Miami area has over twenty-five public parks with tennis courts that are managed by the Miami-Dade County Parks and Recreation Department.

Horses warming up at Hialeah Race Track. Listed on the National Register of Historic Places, Hialeah is considered one of the grand dames of thoroughbred racing facilities complete with old-fashioned grandstands, lush tropical gardens, a clubhouse, and one of the best thoroughbred racing libraries in the United States. Back in its heyday of the 1920s and 1930s, Hialeah attracted socialites, politicians, movie stars, and sports celebrities. Sports writer John Crittenden, who wrote a history of the racetrack, once said that compared to Hialeah, playing the horses at other tracks was "like shooting craps in the back of a filling station." According to Eliot Kleinberg's Historical Traveler's Guide to Florida, Hialeah was the first track in the country to use a photo-finish camera, and the first to use the system in which the money bet set the odds for a race. Home to Miami-Dade County's largest concentration of Cubans, the city of Hialeah, where the track is located, was created in the 1920s as an entertainment center with the racetrack as its main attraction.

A casual round of golf at the Doral Golf Resort and Spa. Home to seven different courses including the Blue Monster—rated one of the top twenty-five in the country—the Doral hosts several world-class tournaments such as the Doral-Ryder Open, which annually launches the PGA Tour. With the Jim McLean Golf School and a golf museum right on the premises, the Doral attracts serious golfers all year long who come to smooth out flaws in their game. Through the years the resort has attracted golf legends such as Ben Hogan, Sam Snead, Arnold Palmer, Jack Nicklaus, Severiano Ballesteros, and Greg Norman. In addition to the Doral, Miami has a variety of nine- and eighteen-hole golf courses at other resorts, country clubs, and public parks. Golf in the Miami area can be traced back to the 1890s when railroad magnate Henry Flagler built the Royal Palm Hotel in what is now downtown Miami. To attract wealthy tourists, he added a six-hole course, and soon after snowbirds flocked down to play. By the 1920s, Miami had established itself as a well-regarded winter haven for avid golfers from the North.

A picture-perfect day at the beach. Out-of-towners are often awestruck by the broad vistas that are common in Miami. But clear blue skies, playful cloud formations, an occasional rainbow, and a view that seems to go on forever are taken for granted by those who live here.

Miami Dolphin fans root for the home team at Pro Player Stadium. Originally built by former Miami Dolphins owner Joe Robbie and formerly named Joe Robbie Stadium, Pro Player is home to both the Florida Marlins and the Miami Dolphins. Some attempts have been made to lend this large football facility a degree of traditional baseball character when the Marlins play. Seating capacity is limited to just over forty thousand for baseball games (as compared to seventy-three thousand for football games) by withdrawing many of the upper-deck and left-field seats from sale. Site of the 1999 Super Bowl, Pro Player is a state-of-the-art, open-air venue that is also used for concerts.

A relaxed Miami Heat Coach Pat Riley signs autographs at a community fundraiser on Miami Beach. Sporting Armani suits and slicked-back hair, Riley is often spotted cruising around town. The second-winningest coach in NBA history, Riley hopes to bring an NBA Championship to the city and has worked hard at toughening up the relatively young team and elevating the franchise to the upper echelon of NBA teams. "My family and I have fallen in love with Miami," Riley once said. "And we hope this will be the final destination of a long coaching journey."

An optimistic Florida Marlins fan hopes for a comeback. Since their first game against the Los Angeles Dodgers in 1993, the Marlins have brought great pride to Miami. And when the brazen young team won the World Series on October 26, 1997, euphoria swept through the city. But the following year, when team owner Wayne Huizenga started trading off the team's best players, the great baseball bubble burst. Although still hopeful for a return to glory, most local fans readily admit that the team has gone from champs to chumps.

A windsurfer catches a breeze. Calm waters and constant winds make Biscayne Bay a popular windsurfing spot. On Key Biscayne, numerous rental shops line the shore, and most offer lessons for beginners. On windy weekends, the waters in this area bustle with brightly colored sails.

Right, top: *A fully rigged sport-fishing boat is ready to reel in the big one. Throughout Miami, deep-sea fishing is a popular diversion for both locals and tourists, and there are hundreds of fishing boats available for charter. Some charge by the hour, others by the day. Most provide bait, tackle, refreshments, and someone to remove the catch from the hook for you. A few of them use electronic fish-finding equipment, while most just rely on old-fashioned know-how. Although not as good as it was twenty years ago, fishing the waters just off the coast still produces plenty of pompano, grouper, snapper, mackerel, sailfish, marlin, tuna, dolphin, bluefish, red-fish, snook, and the occasional shark. The type of fish caught varies with the time of year. Fishing is also popular from bridges, piers, and in the surf, and freshwater fishing is available in the nearby Everglades.*

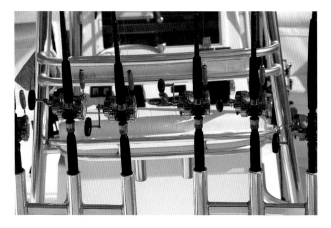

Right, bottom: *Full throttle ahead. Each winter, the Miami International Boat Show attracts hundreds of thousands of boat lovers to the city. Held at the Miami Beach Convention Center and at various marinas in the area, it's one of the biggest in the country and includes crafts of all sizes and types from domestic and international boat manufacturers.*

Late-afternoon libations at Sunday's on the Bay. A favorite watering hole of boaters, Sunday's is a lively eatery on Key Biscayne. With a relaxed Caribbean atmosphere that makes you think of an old Jimmy Buffett song, it features lively reggae bands, fresh seafood, and potent rum cocktails.

Above left: *Stone crab claws with a side of mustard sauce. Plump, rich, and firm, stone crabs are a part of Miami's epicurean identity. In some restaurants, such as Joe's Stone Crab on Miami Beach, patient diners wait in line for hours before being seated. Also served chilled, stone crab is best when fresh and in season—October through May; the rest of the year they are frozen.*

Above right: *Dinner at Versailles Restaurant. On Calle Ocho (Eighth Street) in Little Havana, Versailles is the quintessential Cuban eatery with a wonderfully gaudy décor of crystal chandeliers and wall-to-wall mirrors. Lunchtime is very popular with local business executives who come to cut deals, as well as with families. The mammoth menu features home-style Cuban cooking at its best: garlic-laden roast pork, fried plantains, black bean soup,* arroz con pollo, *fried whole fish, tamales, and sweet caramel flan and café Cubano for dessert.*

A puppeteer entertains the crowds at Bayside Marketplace. With its warm weather and open-arms welcome, Miami attracts many street artists who come to have fun while earning a living. In a typical week, it's not uncommon to come across Peruvian flautists, Haitian drummers, Trinidadian steel pan players, mimes, human robots, and a man who paints his body silver from head to toe and poses as a statue.

Weighing in at eight thousand pounds (3,630 kg), Lolita the Killer Whale loves to swim on her back, wave her tail, and drench onlookers by doing belly flops around her pool. The star attraction of the Miami Seaquarium, Lolita is just one of many reasons to visit this thirty-five-acre (14-hectare) bayfront marine park. Founded in 1955, the Seaquarium is one of the world's finest oceanariums, and is dedicated to the research and preservation of sea life, working closely with its neighbor, the University of Miami's Rosensteil School of Marine and Atmospheric Sciences. The Seaquarium's manatee breeding program, the world's first, has produced many manatees conceived and born in captivity. The Seaquarium has also been successful at hatching green sea turtles, which are on the endangered species list. Along with Lolita, Salty the Sea Lion, and about ten bottlenose dolphins that perform a water ballet, the Seaquarium offers dozens of educational exhibits that feature manatees, stingrays, sharks, hundreds of species of tropical fish, exotic birds, and a rain forest display.

Russian pianist Polina Osetinskaya performs with the Miami Chamber Symphony at the Gusman Concert Hall on the University of Miami campus. A professional orchestra that often hosts internationally acclaimed soloists, the Miami Chamber Symphony regularly offers inexpensive concerts from October through May.

Above: *Behind floor-to-ceiling windows on Lincoln Road, a Miami City Ballet dancer warms up and works through her repertoire at the company's headquarters. Under the artistic direction of Edward Villella, the George Balanchine–trained former star performer with the New York City Ballet, the company has gained international acclaim since its debut in 1985 for its distinctly Latin-flavored style that combines classical ballet with bits of tango and jazz. Although it tours throughout the United States, the Miami City Ballet performs in south Florida from September through April.*

Right, top: *Touted as holding the oldest liquor license in Miami, Tobacco Road near downtown is one of the city's most popular jazz and blues bars. Dark, smoky, and authentically down-home, the bar is decorated with memorabilia from days gone by and old newspaper clippings about performers who have played at the club. Late afternoon brings Brickell Avenue business executives who want to unwind at happy hour, and late at night, the club fills up with music lovers who come for the local and national acts.*

Right, bottom: *Lovers enjoying a sunset kiss on the beach. One of the country's favorite romantic getaways, Miami is an uninhibited destination that's ideal for a passionate tryst. Throughout the city, bartenders playfully hawk the white rum, lemon juice, triple sec, and brandy cocktail known as between-the-sheets. Restaurants serve oysters on the half shell and coconut kiss candies. And hotels offer private hot tubs and champagne on ice.*

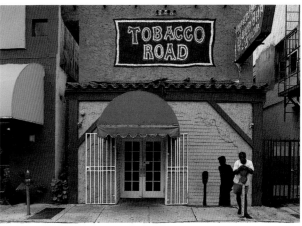

A Tapestry of People and Places

"As mayor of Miami Beach, your day encompasses breakfast with elderly Hispanics, an appearance at an Orthodox Jewish function, and then a gay fundraiser."
—Neisen Kasdin, Miami Beach mayor

Above: *The grand old Biltmore Hotel in Coral Gables. Opened in 1926, the Biltmore in its first incarnation was a dazzling property that catered to wealthy industrialists, royalty, gangsters such as Al Capone, and movie stars—Esther Williams and Tarzan star Johnny Weissmuller used to perform aquatic shows in the pool. Similar to downtown's Freedom Tower, the hotel's tower was also modeled after the five-hundred-year-old Giralda tower in Spain. During World War II, the hotel was transformed into an army hospital caring for wounded and dying soldiers. Some say their spirits still roam the halls, and now a resident storyteller recounts ghost stories in the hotel's lobby every Thursday night. Vacant for decades, the eighteen-story Biltmore was completely remodeled in the late 1980s and opened as an elegant hotel once again. Today, it is on the National Register of Historic Places and attracts visiting politicians, movie stars, authors, athletes, and regular tourists who find its charms hard to resist.*

Facing page: *A young girl in Little Haiti happy to arrive home from school. Miami-Dade County's public school system is the fourth largest in the United States after New York, Los Angeles, and Chicago. There are 201 elementary schools, 51 middle schools, 32 senior high schools, 18 alternative schools, and 7 charter schools in the district with a total of 352,000 students attending kindergarten to twelfth grade. Twenty-six percent of these students are foreign born.*

A worker in Little Haiti on his way home after a long day. Although pockets of exorbitant wealth are abundant in Miami, the socioeconomic gap between local citizens is wide. About one-fourth of all Miami-Dade County residents live below the poverty level.

Near right: *At the University of Miami, Gloria Estefan reads a tribute to salsa singer Celia Cruz before awarding her an honorary degree. Born in Havana in 1957, Estefan left Cuba with her family in 1958 and has become Miami's favorite home-grown success story. Her father was one of many Cuban-Americans captured by the Cuban government during the Bay of Pigs invasion. A graduate of the University of Miami, Estefan made recording history when her 1985 hit song "Conga" appeared on four different pop charts at once. The Grammy award–winning performer raised money for victims of Hurricane Andrew in 1992 by giving a benefit concert and is often spotted walking along Lincoln Road on Miami Beach.*

Far right: *Tête-à-tête on Miami Beach. With its live-and-let-live attitude, South Beach has established itself as a gay-friendly destination. Here, same sex couples can check into a gay hotel, dance at a gay nightclub, and hold hands in public without attracting looks of scorn. Businesses owned or operated by gays often place a pink dot in their storefront window as a symbol of welcome. There's even a well-established gay chamber of commerce and several support groups to help gay newcomers to the area.*

Left, top: *Model behavior on Ocean Drive. With over thirty-five modeling agencies in the Miami area, visitors are often treated to sights like this. Runway beauties are spotted all over town throughout the year primping and posing for fashion photographers. Huge air-conditioned motor homes often line the streets and serve as changing rooms for the strikingly beautiful models—both men and women. The fashion photography business has grown so large in the past ten years that it now generates over $100 million a year for the community, with magazines such as* Vogue *and* Harper's Bazaar *vying for the coveted oceanfront shooting location. The movie business has also grown to be quite large; Miami is now being called Hollywood East because so many major motion pictures have been filmed here. Many local residents have profited by renting out their homes or backyards to film crews earning as much as $3,000 a day. According to the Miami-Dade Office of Film, Television and Print, the movie and entertainment industry annually generates about $1 billion for the local economy.*

Left, bottom: *In Miami, even toddlers wear shades. Located in America's sunbelt, and the southern tip of the "Sunshine State," Miami sees the sun almost 365 days a year. And in July and August, the sun's light can be so bright and so white that it's almost painful to walk around outside without some dark-tinted sunglasses.*

"The people who don't like our diversity have left. The ones staying want this to be a better place."
—Alex Penelas, Mayor, Miami-Dade County, in the *Miami Herald,* January 31, 1999

The Dinner Key Marina in Coconut Grove. During the 1930s and 1940s, the Pan American Seaplane Base and Terminal, which at the time was the busiest seaplane terminal in the United States serving about fifty thousand passengers a year, was located here. In 1943, President Franklin D. Roosevelt flew from the terminal to the Casablanca Conference with British Prime Minister Winston Churchill; during World War II, it served as a U.S. Navy base. The city of Miami bought the property from Pan Am in 1946 for use as a waterfront park. Today it is one of the largest and most desirable marinas in Miami, with a long waiting list for available slips, and harbors both commercial fishing boats and privately owned live-aboard sailboats and yachts.

A private residence on Palm Island. The former home of gangster Al Capone, Palm Island is now a very quiet and subdued residential community in Miami Beach. Connected to the north side of the MacArthur Causeway by a small bridge, it is one of the most exclusive and expensive neighborhoods in Miami.

Left: *At the northern tip of Miami-Dade County, the city of North Miami Beach is marked by dozens of towering, modern condominiums like this one. Condo Canyon, as it is called, is home to Turnberry Isle Resort and the sprawling Aventura Mall. In the late 1990s, a local burglar nicknamed Spider Man operated in the area, scaling tall buildings like this with his bare hands, breaking into balconies, and walking off—or rather climbing down—with sacks of precious jewelry.*

Below: *The elite private enclave known as Fisher Island. In 1925, local developer Carl Fisher traded this island at the southern tip of Miami Beach to William K. Vanderbilt II in exchange for a 220-foot (67-meter) yacht. Vanderbilt built a mansion complete with huge marble fireplaces on the island, and that grand home is now the centerpiece restaurant and club of this exclusive community. Accessible only by ferry, the 216-acre Fisher Island contains several condominiums and cottages, a nine-hole golf course, private beach, European-style spa, tennis courts, and a deep-water marina. There are very few cars on the island, and residents and guests—by invitation only—get around in golf carts. One of Fisher Island's many well-known residents is talk show host Oprah Winfrey, who flies down for a respite when the Chicago winters get brutal.*

An artist bikes along with Miami Beach traffic. Drawn by the low studio rents and relaxed quality of life, hundreds of artists have moved to the city in the past decade. Many have come from Haiti or Latin America in search of opportunity; others just escaped the fast pace of life in New York.

A colorful street mural. In various neighborhoods in Miami—Little Haiti, Coconut Grove, South Beach—street art is abundant. So vibrant is the local art scene here that several area artists have attracted national attention—Cuban-born José Bedia and Haitian-born Edouard Duval-Carrie among them—and Christie's, the famed art auction house, recently opened a branch in Miami.

"Delving into Miami's ethnic dynamics is not an excursion into the world of quaint foreign customs and interesting immigrant subcultures at the margins of the city's mainstream. Rather, it is to reach into what has become the soul of Miami. Ethnicity is at the core of Miami's uniqueness."
—Dr. Lisandro Perez, Director of Cuban Research Institute, Florida International University

Above: *Gyory Art Studio in the Miami Design District. Located a few miles north of downtown Miami, the neighborhood known as the Design District has become in the past decade a creative enclave of art and photography galleries, antique shops, and home and design showrooms. Many artists and designers have moved into the area transforming rundown apartments into upscale lofts. On the second Friday of each month, the District hosts a gallery night with walking tours of all the shops. And one of the most interesting spots in the area is Power Studios, a bohemian collection of restaurants and music clubs that feature live Brazilian, Haitian, Afro-Cuban, and jazz acts on weekends.*

Left, top: *The Alhambra Water Tower in Coral Gables. The city was intentionally designed to evoke a Spanish Mediterranean atmosphere, and the streets in Coral Gables were named after cities in Spain. Among them: Giralda, Segovia, Toledo, Madrid, Catalonia, Minorca, Aragon, Seville, Andalusia, and Cortez.*

Left, bottom: *A parishioner on her way home from the Cathedral of St. Mary in Little Haiti. Little Haiti is a classic juxtaposition of immigrant optimism and inner-city problems. Miami's Haitian community has a population of fifty thousand residents, many of whom fled their poverty-stricken homeland in fragile wooden boats. Covering about two hundred square blocks, the neighborhood of Little Haiti lies a few miles northwest of downtown Miami and is full of Haitian grocery stores, record shops, and small mom-and-pop restaurants. Houses are painted bright Caribbean colors, and commercial signs are in French and Creole. Not far from the Cathedral of St. Mary is the Toussaint Louverture Elementary School, named after the Haitian national hero who led a peasant uprising against the French. The architectural focal point of the neighborhood is the Caribbean Marketplace on Northeast Second Avenue. This open-air, gabled-roof building painted bright yellow, blue, green, and orange, was designed to resemble the historic Iron Market in Port-au-Prince, Haiti, and was granted the prestigious National Honor Award by the American Institute of Architects in 1991. Intended to be a cultural and commercial meeting place for the community, the Marketplace, however, has fallen on hard times.*

Right: *The seemingly lost art of handmade cigars is still alive and well at El Credito Cigar Factory, which is hidden away in a tiny storefront on Calle Ocho (Eighth Street) in Little Havana. Founded in Cuba in 1907, El Credito moved to Miami in the early 1960s, but the nostalgic setting of the shop feels more like the 1940s—bathing-beauty pictures of Betty Grable still hang on the walls. The heady aroma of to-bacco hangs in the air and the sounds of Spanish radio programs blare in the back-ground. El Credito remains the largest cigar factory in the city, and visitors are al-ways welcome to come in and watch doz-ens of cigarmakers stretch, dry, chop, and roll tobacco leaves into thick stogies. In ad-dition to the cigar factories, Miami has doz-ens of exclusive cigar shops and private smokers clubs that cater to cigar aficiona-dos.*

Below, left: *A young Miccosukee woman. At the Miccosukee Indian Reservation west of Miami, Florida's native inhabitants wel-come visitors and offer interpretive tours that explain their history, culture, language, and relationship with the land.*

Below, right: *Fooling around at the shore. In addition to the beach, playful places abound for kids in Miami. In fact, to the north of South Beach most of the larger oceanfront hotels are kid friendly and of-fer family packages with special activities, entertainment, sports, and meals just for children.*

Above: *A somber tribute to the tragedies of World War II, the Holocaust Memorial is a forty-two-foot-high (13-meter) bronze sculpture of an outstretched hand reaching toward the sky with life-size renditions of terrified victims struggling to climb to the top. Located on Miami Beach's Meridian Avenue, it was designed by local architect Kenneth Treister and sits inside a reflecting pool full of lily pads. Dedicated to the six million Jews who died in the Nazi concentration camps, it's appropriately located amid one of the largest communities of Holocaust survivors in the world.*

Left: *Jewish residents enjoy a day at the beach. The Jewish community of Miami is vast, vibrant, and well established. After New York and Los Angeles, Miami has the third-largest Jewish community in the country. Historically, Jews have thrived in the city. In the 1960s, Miami's Jewish population exploded due to the large numbers of northern retirees who settled here along with the Cuban Jews fleeing the communist takeover of their island. Later, they were joined by Jewish immigrants from Russia, Poland, Israel, and South America. Today the total Jewish population is about 150,000, but the community itself is very diverse. There are Reformed, Conservative, Orthodox, and Reconstructionist Jews each with their own synagogues and associated organizations. There are Lubavitcher Hasidic Jews, Ashkenazic Jews whose ancestors can be traced to Central and Eastern Europe, and Sephardic Jews with family histories that go back to the Iberian Peninsula. There are also secular Jews with no particular religious affiliation.*

Plymouth Congregational Church in Coconut Grove. Built in 1917, the design for the church was taken from the design of an old city mission church in Mexico, and the 375-year-old, hand-carved wooden front door came from a monastery in the Pyrenees Mountains. A hole in the lower-right side of the door was added a few years after the church opened so that neighborhood cats could enter and take care of the mice that had infested the buildings. Located on Devon Road, the church's ivy-covered coral rock façade is often used as a setting for newlyweds who come to pose for their wedding portraits.

Trying on basic black at a stylish boutique. Listed as the number one thing that tourists love to do while on vacation, shopping in Miami is also a serious diversion for locals. According to the Miami Herald, over four hundred thousand people in south Florida are employed in the retail business, which is more than double the number of people employed in the hotel and restaurant businesses combined.

The horseshoe arches, domes, and minarets typical of the Moorish-revival architecture in the city of Opa-locka. In the northwest quadrant of Miami-Dade County, Opa-locka is one of the area's most economically depressed areas. Inspired by the Arabian Nights stories, aviation pioneer Glenn Curtiss designed the city in 1925 and had dreams of it becoming one of the most affluent planned communities in the country. These days the city hosts an annual Arabian Nights Festival each spring. Also in the city is the Opa-locka Airport, from which Amelia Earhart took off on the first leg of her ill-fated trip around the world in 1937.

The generational divide. Once referred to as God's waiting room because of the large number of elderly people who lived here, the city of Miami Beach is no longer a retirement haven. Today the median age is a youthful forty-four years old, the median family income is twenty-two thousand dollars, and the number of residents who are fourteen years old or younger continues to rise. While there is still a substantial number of retirees who live here, more and more young singles and couples with small children are choosing to make their homes in Miami Beach, totally transforming the atmosphere of the neighborhood.

In Little Havana, a bronze map of Cuba washed over by flowing water honors José Martí, poet, philosopher, and leader of the Cuban struggle to gain independence from Spain. Today, José Martí is still revered by Cubans in Cuba and in Miami. A park near the Miami River in Little Havana is dedicated in his name.

Above: *Created by artist Tony Lopez, this life-size bronze statue is a tribute to Nestor "Tony" Izquierdo, a soldier who fought in the Bay of Pigs invasion of Cuba. The statue is located on Cuban Memorial Boulevard in Little Havana, not far from the Eternal Torch of Brigade 2506, a memorial to the ninety-four Cuban exiles who died in the foiled invasion. Sponsored by the CIA, the 1961 invasion was intended to spark an uprising among the Cuban people and topple Fidel Castro, but it failed. Almost one thousand men were taken prisoner by the Cuban government, and the rest retreated to Miami.*

Left: *A traditional, bride-wears-white Catholic wedding. In recent years, Miami—and especially Miami Beach—has become a "wedding destination." Lovesick tourists fly in, apply for a marriage license at City Hall, and are quickly married by a local judge.*

Listed in the phone book under religious goods, botanicas are living testimony that the Afro-Caribbean religions of Voodoo and Santería are thriving in Miami. Whether you want to cast a spell, or just look around, a visit to a botanica will introduce you to an array of exotic potions—aromatic roots, virility pills, powdered bulls' horns, floor polish to ward off evil spirits, and ready-made voodoo dolls equipped with pins. Both Voodoo and Santería have their roots in the religions of the Yoruba tribes of Western Africa and were brought to the Caribbean by slaves. When the island masters forced the slaves to adopt Christianity, the religions took on a Christian character, but one with a distinct animistic and pantheistic tone. Both Santería and Voodoo were brought to Miami by the Caribbean immigrants who settled here. Although they are found throughout the city, botanicas are most common in Little Haiti and Little Havana.

A machete is the best tool for opening a coconut. This large, oblong, green nut is what a coconut looks like when it hangs on a tree; the small, hairy brown husk is hidden underneath the green shell, with the rich white fruit hidden inside the hairy brown shell. Sometimes street vendors hack them open and insert a straw to drink the clear, sweetish "coconut water." Frequently confused with this clear water, coconut milk is actually a man-made concoction created by mixing freshly grated coconut meat with boiling water, pureeing it in a blender, and then straining it through cheesecloth. Coconut milk is commonly used in Miami to cook rice, curries, fish, chicken, desserts, and candies.

"Miami is the only city in America where you
can advocate the violent overthrow of a foreign
government in a church."
—Tom Miller, author

Above: *Commodore Plaza in Coconut Grove. After several years of being outshined by its trendy, Art-Deco-on-steroids South Beach sister, the neighborhood of Coconut Grove is once again a popular spot. Located a few miles south of downtown, the Grove is one of the oldest and most diverse neighborhoods in Miami. Originally a haven for relocated New Englanders, the Grove at one time or another has been a nucleus for artists, poets, gays, drug dealers, boat captains, beatniks, hippies, and yuppies. After languishing during the 1980s, it underwent a renaissance in the 1990s that injected a born-again spirit into its collective unconscious, and its streets are now full of outdoor cafés, restaurants, art galleries, boutiques, bookstores, antique shops, and comedy clubs. Although it does suffer from a terminal case of what many call ostentatious development, the Grove still has an eclectic, diverse atmosphere where young and old, rich and poor, black and white, Cubans and Jews, Rastafarians and Hare Krishnas mingle as one. It's also home to the Coconut Grove Playhouse, an intimate eleven-hundred-seat theater built in 1926. And each February it hosts the Coconut Grove Arts Festival, one of the largest outdoor art shows in the country.*

Right: *A relaxing game of bocci on Key Biscayne. The traditional Old World Italian game of lawn bowling, bocci doesn't take great athletic ability, and is surprisingly popular with Latinos in Miami.*

Facing page: *Clad in caps and gowns, three college students celebrate their graduation from the University of Miami. Sometimes called a melting pot, other times called a tossed salad where each ingredient retains its original flavor, Miami's multicultural makeup ensures a rich experience for all who live here.*

Index

African-American community, 11–12
Alhambra Water Tower, 85
American Airlines, 21, 27
Arabian Nights Festival, 89
Arquitectonica, 24, 26
Art Deco District, 49, 52, 56
Art Deco hotels, 10, 13, 52, 58, 63
Art Deco style, 10, 13, 52, 61, 63
Art Deco Weekend, 56
Art Moderne style, 52
artistic community, 53, 84
Atlantis condominium, 24
Aventura Mall, 83
Bal Harbour, 40
Ballet Flamenco La Rosa, 65
banking, 26
banyan trees, 43
Barry, Dave, 23, 49
Bash, 66
Bay of Pigs invasion, 11, 90
Bayfront Park, 19
Bayfront Park Amphitheater, 19
Bayside Marketplace, 17, 19, 29, 76
Bedia, José, 84
Bee Gees, The, 67
bicycling, 31
Big Fish, 28
Bill Baggs Cape Florida State Recreation Area, 46
Biltmore Hotel, 45, 79
Biscayne Bay, 19, 74
Biscayne National Park, 39
black beans, 44
bocci, 92
body art, 56
botanicas, 91
Breakwater Hotel, 58
Brickell Avenue, 8, 24
Brickell, William B., 8
Buchanan, Edna, 12, 31, 49
building boom, 15
café Cubano, 22
Café Nostalgia, 67
Calle Ocho (party during Carnivale Miami), 68
Calle Ocho (street), 67, 75, 86
Cape Florida, see Bill Baggs Cape Florida State Recreation Area
Cape Florida Lighthouse, 46
Capone, Al, 15, 79, 82
Carboney, M., 2
Caribbean Marketplace, 85
Carnivale Miami, 68
Casa Casuarina, 60
Castro, Fidel, 10–11, 13, 19, 90
Cathedral of St. Mary in Little Haiti, 85
cats, 23
China Grill, 61
Christ of the Deep statue, 39
cigarmakers, 86
Claude and Mildred Pepper Fountain, 24
Clevelander Hotel, 63
Coconut Grove, 8, 32, 40, 67, 69, 70, 88, 92

Coconut Grove Arts Festival, 92
Coconut Grove Playhouse, 92
coconuts, 91
Columbus Day Regatta, 46
Commodore Plaza, 92
conga line, world's longest, 68
Coral Gables, 10, 27, 31, 37, 39, 40, 43, 45, 85
Coral Gables Congregational Church, 12
Crittenden, John, 71
Cuban Missile Crisis, 11
Cuban refugees, 10–11, 18, 19, 54
Cuban-American community, 11, 13, 71
Dade County Courthouse, 18
Dade, Major Francis L., 8
Dade Massacre, 8
Deering, James, 10, 32
Delano Hotel, 57, 63
demographics of Miami, 8, 13, 27, 89
Design District, 85
Dinner Key Marina, 82
disco dancing, 67
Doral Golf Resort and Spa, 39, 72
Doral-Ryder Open, 72
drug smuggling, 12
Duval-Carrie, Edouard, 84
Eden Roc Hotel, 10
El Credito Cigar Factory, 86
elderly population, 89
Estefan, Gloria, 13, 29, 68, 80
ethnic mix, 8, 13
Everglades National Park, 39
Fairchild Tropical Garden, 31
Fifth Street Gym, 61
Fisher Island, 83
fishing, 74
Flagler, Henry M., 8, 72
flamenco dancing, 65
flamingos, 46
Florida Marlins, 73
Fontainebleau Hilton Resort and Towers, 58
food, 68–69
    see also specific types of food
Fort Lauderdale/Hollywood International Airport, 21
Freedom Tower, 18
gambling,
    Miccosukee Resort and Convention Center, 34
    offshore, 20
gay community, 80
Gesu Catholic Church, 28
golfing, 72
guarapo, 43
Gusman Center for the Performing Arts, 29
Gusman Concert Hall, 76
Gyory Art Studio, 85
Haitian cuisine, 67
Hard Rock Café, 17, 19, 29
Hemingway, Ernest, 21, 66
Hialeah Race Track, 46, 71
Hispanic population, 27
Historical Museum of Southern Florida, 18
Holocaust Memorial, 87
Homestead, 44
Huizenga, Wayne, 73
Hurricane Andrew, 13, 26, 32, 35, 42
hurricanes, 42
    1926, 10
    1935, 10

    see also Hurricane Andrew
ibis, 35
immigration, 13
    Cubans, 10–11, 12
    Haitians, 11
    South and Central Americans, 12
    see also Mariel Boatlift
Intercontinental Bank, 26
International Tennis Center, 71
Italian Renaissance Festival, 32
Izquierdo, Nestor "Tony", 90
Jewish community, 10, 54, 87
Jim McLean Golf School, 72
Joe's Stone Crab, 75
John Pennekamp Coral Reef State Park, 39
Johnson, Philip, 18
KC and the Sunshine Band, 67
Key Biscayne, 11, 31, 40, 46, 71, 74, 75
King Mango Strut, 70
King Orange Jamboree Parade, 65
language, 27
Lapidus, Morris, 58
Leslie Hotel, 2
Liberty City Riots of 1980, 12
Lincoln Road, 56, 77
Lipton International Players Championship, 71
literary community, 49
Little Haiti, 85
Little Havana, 11, 67, 68, 75, 86, 89, 90
lobsters, 22
Loews Miami Beach Hotel, 50
Lopez, Tony, 90
MacArthur Causeway, 15, 82
Mandela, Nelson, 13
mangos, 43
Mango's Tropical Café, 66
Mariel Boatlift, 12
Martí, José, 89
Metromover, 23
Metrorail, 23
Miami Art Museum, 18
Miami Beach, 8, 10, 49, 50, 50, 75, 87
    see also Art Deco District; Miami Beach
    Convention Center; North Miami Beach; South
    Beach
Miami Beach Convention Center, 50, 74
Miami Chamber Symphony, 76
Miami Circle, 23
Miami City Ballet, 77
Miami Dolphins, 11, 24, 27, 73
Miami Heat, 73
Miami Herald, 23
Miami International Airport (MIA), 21
Miami International Boat Show, 74
Miami International Book Fair, 49
Miami International Film Festival, 29
Miami Museum of Science and Space Transit
    Planetarium, 70
Miami River, 7, 8, 21
Miami Seaquarium, 76
Miami Vice, 12, 24, 49
Miami/Bahamas Goombay Festival, 69
Miami-Dade Cultural Center, 18
Miami-Dade Main Library, 18
Miccosukee Indians, 34, 86
    patchwork fabric, 7
Miccosukee Indian Reservation, 34, 86
Miccosukee Indian Village, 34

Miccosukee Indian Village Resort and Convention
    Center, 34
modeling, 81
Munroe, Ralph M., 8
murals, street, 84
music, 28, 61
NationsBank Tower, 24
New World Cuisine, 43
New World Symphony, 23
News Café, 60, 61
Noguchi, Isamu, 19
North Miami Beach, 83
Ocean Drive, 13, 49, 56, 61, 63
Opa-locka, 89
Orange Bowl Stadium, 27
Orchid Jungle, 35
paella, 68, 69
Palace Condominium, 26
Palm Island, 82
Pan Am Air Bridge, 21
Pan American Seaplane Base and Terminal, 82
parks and recreation areas, 39
    see also Bill Baggs Cape Florida State
    Recreation Area; Biscayne National Park;
    Everglades National Park
Parrot Jungle, 45
Pei, I. M., 24
Penelas, Mayor Alex, 81
plantains, 7
Plymouth Congregational Church, 88
Ponce de León, Juan, 8
population, 8

Port of Miami, 10
    cargo exports from, 20
    cruise ships, 15
poverty, 80
Power Studios, 85
Pro Player Stadium, 73
Redland, 44
Rickenbacker Causeway, 31
Riley, Pat, 73
Roosevelt, Franklin D., 24, 82
Rosensteil School of Marine and Atmospheric
    Sciences, 76
Sanford L. Ziff Jewish Museum, 54
Santería, 91
Scarface, 24
schools, 79
Scull, Haydee and Sahara, 53
seashells, 37
Secada, John, 29
Seminoles, 8, 21, 34
Sheraton Bal Harbour Beach Resort, 40
shipping, 20, 21
shopping, 17, 55, 88
snakes, as pets, 70
Somoza Debayle, Anastasio, 12
South Beach, 50, 52, 53, 54, 55, 56, 80
Spanish exploration of Florida, 8
St. Moritz Hotel, 60
Starck, Philippe, 63
stone crab, 75
street performers, 76
Summit of the Americas, 13

Sunday's on the Bay, 75
Tap Tap, 67
Tobacco Road, 77
tours,
    by boats, 20
    by planes, 21
tourism, 12, 13, 49, 53
Toussaint Louverture Elementary School, 85
transportation, public, 23
Treister, Kenneth, 87
Turnberry Isle Resort, 83
Tuttle, Julia, 8
University of Miami, 10, 27, 35
    see also Gusman Concert Hall; Rosensteil
    School of Marine and Atmospheric Sciences
Vanderbilt II, William K., 83
Venetian Pool, 37
Versace, Gianni, 13, 60
Versailles Restaurant, 75
Villa Regina, 26
violence in Miami, 12
    murder of Gianni Versace, 13
    tourist shootings, 13, 60
Vizcaya Museum and Gardens, 10, 13, 32
Voodoo, 91
weather, 57
windsurfing, 74
Winfrey, Oprah, 83

Where to Go for More Information

Greater Miami Convention & Visitors Bureau
Suite 2400
701 Brickell Avenue
Miami, FL 33131
(305) 539-3000 or 800-283-2707
www.miamiandbeaches.com

Florida Division of Tourism
P.O. Box 1100
Tallahassee, FL 32302
(904) 487-1462
www.flausa.com

About the Author and Photographer

Author Joann Biondi, a Miami resident since 1974, has published ten books on topics ranging from Africa to Cuba to her present home city, along with numerous magazine and newspaper stories on Europe, South America, the Caribbean, and South Florida. Her travel articles on Miami and its vast cultural diversity have appeared in the *New York Times, Travel & Leisure, Caribbean Travel & Life,* and *Conde Naste Traveler.* As an adjunct professor at Miami-Dade Community College and Florida International University, Biondi teaches Cultural Geography and the Sociology of Leisure.

Photograph © Maria La Yacona

Photographer Tony Arruza was born in Cuba and has lived in south Florida since coming to the United States in 1960 at the age of seven. He has published eight books, including *Florida* (Compass American Guides) and *The Smithsonian Guide to Natural America: The Southeast*. His work has also appeared in *Audubon, Food and Wine, Islands, Men's Journal, Golf Digest,* National Geographic books, *Newsweek,* the *New York Times, Outside, Salt Water Sportsman, Surfing, Travel Holiday,* and *Travel & Leisure.*

Photograph © Michael Price